Grammar Three

Jennifer Seidl

Oxford University Press

Contents

1 Are you running away? Present simple or present continuous

JENNY What's wrong? **Are** you **running** away from something?

JANE Yes, a horrible green lizard on a skateboard **is chasing** me.

JENNY That isn't a lizard. That's Trig, an alien from Triglon. He's very friendly.

JANE **I don't care** who he is, **I don't like** him. **I don't** usually **talk** to aliens. Merton is a very strange town.

JENNY Are you new here?

JANE Yes. **I live** in Kingsley, but my brother Ben and **I are staying** with my Aunt Sarah and my cousin Mike for a few months. I haven't got any friends here.

JENNY Well, **I'm going** to the cinema with my brother tonight. Do you want to come?

JANE Yes, thanks. **I love** films . . . But **is** Trig **coming**?

Grammar lesson

Present simple

We use the present simple

- for things that repeatedly happen (or don't happen) especially with **always, often, usually, sometimes, never, every day** etc.:
  ▶ *I don't usually **talk** to aliens.*

- for things and facts which do not usually change:
  ▶ *I **live** in Kingsley.*

- with verbs such as **like, love, hate, dislike, know, believe, think**:
  ▶ *I **love** films.*

Present continuous

We use the present continuous

- for something that is happening at the moment of speaking, often with **now, at the moment, today** etc.:
  ▶ *A green lizard **is chasing** me.*
  *Are you **running** away from something?*

- for something that is happening for a limited time in the present:
  ▶ *I'm **staying** in Merton for a few months.*

- to talk about future plans, often with time expressions such as **next week, on Tuesday, tonight**:
  ▶ *We're **going** to the cinema tonight.*
  *Is Trig **coming**?*

1 Make them fit

Fit the **he/she/it** forms of these verbs in the present simple into the puzzle.

do	be	begin
hurry	have	mix ✓

Fit the **ing** forms of these verbs into the puzzle.

forget	choose ✓	hit
lie	make	happen

2 What's happening?

Debbie Foster is returning to Merton. She has won an Olympic medal for swimming. What's happening? Use the verbs from the box in the present continuous to complete the sentences.

come ✓	get out	enter
stop	try	ride
shake	stand	wave

▶ Now the car _is coming_ round the corner.

1 Two policemen on motor bikes _____ in front of the car.

2 A policeman _____ the traffic.

3 Some people _____ flags.

4 Now Debbie _____ of the car.

5 The Mayor _____ hands with her.

6 Now Debbie _____ the town hall.

7 Jenny and Nick _____ to see what's happening.

8 Trig _____ on Nick's shoulders.

3 Do you watch too much television?

These people were asked if they watched too much television. Here are their answers.

Yes, I think I do. I'm a cartoon fan. I never miss a single one. I spend three or four hours a day in front of the TV.

MAX

No, I don't. I have other things to do. I play the piano and read. I watch nature programmes, but I don't usually know what's on TV.

MARION

I don't think that I watch too much TV. I watch for about an hour a day. I like video clips but I think game shows are stupid. I read the TV guide from cover to cover, so I always know what's on.

DAVE

Yes, I do. As soon as I come home from school I turn on the TV. I sometimes watch for about five hours a day. My Mum doesn't say anything. I do my homework in the mornings when I'm fresh.

JILL

a   Say if these sentences are true or false. Correct the false statements.

▶   Max watches cartoons.
    True.
▶   Marion watches game shows.
    False. She doesn't watch game shows.
1   Dave likes video clips.
2   Marion watches TV for three or four hours a day.
3   Jill plays the piano.
4   Max never misses a single cartoon.
5   Jill does her homework in the evenings.
6   Marion reads the TV guide from cover to cover.
7   Dave watches TV for an hour a day.
8   Max hates cartoons.
9   Jill phones her friends when she comes home from school.
10 Dave spends five hours a day in front of the TV.
11 Max watches TV for an hour a day.
12 Dave always knows what's on TV.
13 Marion likes video clips.
14 Dave hates game shows.
15 Max thinks that he watches too much TV.

b   Work with a partner. Ask and answer five questions with **do** or **does**. Give short answers.

▶   YOU   *Does Max watch game shows?*
    PARTNER   *No, he doesn't.*
▶   YOU   *Do Max and Jill watch too much television?*
    PARTNER   *Yes, they do.*

c   Write your own opinion in a short paragraph. Do you watch too much television? What do you like? What don't you like?

I don't watch too much television . . .

4 Detectives at work

Tom and Nick are watching the house across the
street. Something strange is happening.
Put the verbs in brackets in the present simple or the
present continuous to make correct sentences.

TOM   What ▶ *are you staring* (you stare) at?

NICK   There's a man at the Johnsons' house. He
▶ *doesn't live* (not live) there. I wonder
what he <u>1</u> (do).

TOM   Perhaps he <u>2</u> (visit) the Johnsons.

NICK   No. They're not at home. They both <u>3</u>
(work) in town. They <u>4</u> (catch) the
same train as Dad every morning. It's strange. He
<u>5</u> (look) at the house very carefully.

TOM   Now he <u>6</u> (try) to open the gate, but
it's locked. Look! He <u>7</u> (climb) over the
garden wall. I can't see him now.

NICK   Let's follow him. I want to see what he <u>8</u> (do).

TOM   He <u>9</u> (go) to the garage. He
<u>10</u> (carry) a ladder. Now he
<u>11</u> (put) the ladder up to the bedroom
window!

NICK   He must be a burglar . . . Hey! You! What
<u>12</u> (you do)?

MAN   It's all right, boys. I'm an insurance agent. I
<u>13</u> (examine) the storm damage to
the roof. The Johnsons <u>14</u> (know)
that I'm here.

2 Who invented jeans? Past simple or past continuous?

TOM   You've got mud on your jeans.

NICK   So what? The prospectors' jeans **were** much dirtier.

TOM   You mean during the Californian Gold Rush? **Did** they **wear** jeans then?

NICK   They say that the prospectors **were** the first people to wear jeans. They **didn't wear** their best clothes to look for gold, you know.

TOM   Who **invented** jeans?

NICK   Levi Strauss **made** the first pair of jeans in America in 1850. He was a tailor. He **was travelling** from New York to San Francisco, when he **met** some men who **were digging** for gold in a cold, muddy river and . . .

Grammar lesson

Past simple

We form the past simple with **ed** or **d** for regular verbs.

> invent → invent**ed**   live → live**d**

Irregular verbs have a special form. Look at the list at the back of the book.

> wear → **wore**   meet → **met**

We use **did** + infinitive without **to** for questions, and **did not** or **didn't** + infinitive without **to** for the negative.

> ▶ *Did they wear jeans?*
> *They didn't wear their best clothes.*

We use the past simple for an action that started and finished in the past, often with a time expression.

> ▶ *He made the first pair of jeans in America.*

Past continuous

We form the past continuous with **was**/**were** + an **ing** form.

> ▶ *he was travelling*   *they were digging*

We make questions and negative forms like this:

> ▶ *Was he travelling to New York?*
> *He was not* (OR *wasn't*) *travelling to New York.*

We use the past continuous for an action that was already happening at a particular time in the past.

> ▶ *When he met them, they were digging for gold.*

Past simple or past continuous?

When one action interrupts another, we use the past continuous and the past simple together in one sentence.

We use the past continuous (**was travelling**) for the longer action and the past simple (**met**) for the shorter 'interrupting' action.

> ▶ *Levi was travelling from New York to San Francisco when he met some men.*

1 Verb square

How many verbs in the past simple can you find?
Are there fourteen, sixteen or eighteen?

```
W  Q  K  X  C  O  M  E  V (C  A  M  E)
S  E  N  T  M  R  U  N  Q  S  E  E  X
A  R  E  Z  S  A  Y  K  W  E  N  T  Z
W  F  W  E  R  E  X  G  O  T  X  X  Z
G  A  V  E  E  A  J  A  R  B  V  E  H
K  N  O  W  A  T  O  O  K  K  W  A  S
F  O  U  N  D  K  X  X  E  R  A  N  Z
B  R  O  U  G  H  T  Z  D  I  D  K  W
```

2 What were they doing?

Jenny went to a party. When she arrived, this is what she saw.

Work with a partner. Study the picture for one minute, then cover it. Take turns to read the questions and give answers using the past continuous.

▶ Who was standing near the window? A boy
   or a girl?
   A girl was standing near the window.
1 What was the girl near the window doing?
2 How many people were standing near the
   food?
3 What was the girl in the corner doing?

4 What was the girl in the corner wearing?
5 How many people were dancing?
6 Was anybody sitting on the floor?
7 How many people were playing cards?
8 Was anybody sleeping?
9 Who was singing? A boy or a girl?
10 Was anybody drinking cola?

3   How jeans came to America

Put the verbs in brackets in the past simple or past continuous.

Levi Strauss ▶ *came*_____ (come) from a small town in the south
of Germany. When he 1_____ (be) a young man, he
2_____ (fall) in love with the mayor's daughter.
But the mayor and Levi's parents 3_____ (not want)
them to marry.

Levi's parents 4_____ (send) him away to New York where
his brothers 5_____ (live). They 6_____ (be)
tailors and they 7_____ (teach) him to sew.

In 1850, Levi 8_____ (take) some sailcloth from New York
to San Francisco when he 9_____ (meet) some men. They
10_____ (dig) for gold in the streams and rivers. The
weather was bad. It 11_____ (rain) and the wind
12_____ (blow). The men were cold because they
13_____ (wear) only thin trousers.

Suddenly Levi 14_____ (have) an idea. He
15_____ (use) the sailcloth which he
16_____ (transport) to make trousers for the men. Then he
17_____ (sew) on metal studs to make them stronger.

The men 18_____ (love) the trousers but they
19_____ (not like) the yellow-grey colour. So when Levi
Strauss 20_____ (open) a tailor's shop in San Francisco, he
21_____ (import) a special thick blue material from Nimes
in France. That's how jeans 22_____ (become) blue.

4 Where did he come from?

a Use the words in brackets to write questions about Levi Strauss.

▶ He came from Germany. (Where . . . from)
Where did he come from?
_____

1 His parents sent him to America. (Where)
_____

2 His brothers taught him to sew. (What)
_____

3 In 1850 he set out for San Francisco. (When)
_____
_____

4 He met some prospectors on the way. (Who)
_____
_____

5 They were digging in a river. (Where)
_____
_____

6 They were wearing thin trousers. (What)
_____
_____

7 He was taking sailcloth to California. (What)
_____
_____

8 He made trousers from the sailcloth.
(What . . . from)
_____
_____

9 The men didn't like the colour. (Why)
_____
_____

10 He imported blue material from France.
(Where . . . from)
_____
_____

5 A fright

a Read about Jane's frightening experience. Put the verbs in brackets in the past simple or the past continuous.

I ▶ *caught* _____ (catch) the nine o'clock bus home last night. It ▶ *was getting* _____ (get) dark and it ^{1} _____ (rain) hard as well.

When I ^{2} _____ (get off) the bus, there was no one in the street, only an old man who ^{3} _____ (take) his dog for a walk. He ^{4} _____ (walk) in the opposite direction.

Suddenly, I ^{5} _____ (hear) footsteps behind me. I ^{6} _____ (begin) to run but they ^{7} _____ (come) nearer and nearer. I ^{8} _____ (run) faster and faster, and I ^{9} _____ (shake) with fright.

I finally ^{10} _____ (reach) home, but just as I ^{11} _____ (put) the key in the door, I ^{12} _____ (feel) a hand on my shoulder.

A man's voice ^{13} _____ (say), 'Excuse me Miss, here's your umbrella. You ^{14} _____ (leave) it on the bus.'

b Think of an experience or a situation which frightened you. Write a short paragraph about it. Include where you were, what you were doing and what suddenly happened.

Read your story to the class.

3 We've repaired the car

Present perfect simple or present perfect continuous?

JENNY Nick, you're covered with oil. What **have** you **been doing**?

NICK Well, Jane's cousin Mike **has bought** an old car, and it **has been making** strange noises, so we **have been helping** him to repair it. Jane and I **have been working** on it for hours. We**'ve** just **finished**. We**'ve cleaned** all the parts. The engine looks like new.

JENNY But Nick, you **have** never **repaired** a car before . . .

NICK It's easy. And look, **I've found** all these extra screws.

Grammar lesson

Present perfect simple

Form

have or **has** + past participle
▶ *I have finished*   *he has bought*

Look at the back of the book for a list of irregular verbs and their past participles.

Use

We use the present perfect simple

■ for a completed action with **just**, **already** and **yet**:
▶ *We've just finished.*

■ for a completed action which has an effect or result in the present:
▶ *We've cleaned all the parts.*
(result: The engine looks like new.)

■ for a completed action at an unknown or unstated time, often with **ever** and **never**:
▶ *You have never repaired a car before.*

Present perfect continuous

Form

have been or **has been** + ing
▶ *we have been helping*
he has been working

Use

We use the present perfect continuous

■ for an action that begins in the past and continues up to the present. The action may be finished or unfinished:
▶ *The car has been making strange noises.*

■ with **for** and **since** and **how long** to emphasize how long an action has been happening:
▶ *We have been working on it for hours.*

■ often with the long action verbs **play**, **learn**, **do**, **wait**, **live**, **rain**, **work**, **sleep** etc.:
▶ *It has been raining all day.*

1 Ring the past participles

a How many past participles can you find? Be careful! Some words are in the past simple form.

```
(B E E N) X K X D R A W N S
L S A Z Q N Z J U T R S T
O W T F R O Z E N E I P O
W A E X S W U M Y Z T O L
N M N W E N T R A N T K E
T A K E N Q W A S S E E N
F E L L Q D R I V E N N Q
S H A K E N X G O N E Q Z
```

b Round the class, say the infinitive, past simple and past participle forms of the verbs you have found.

infinitive	past simple	past participle
▶ *be*	*was*	*been*

---

2 The race

a Look at what has happened in the race. Read the sentences and put a ✓ to show if they are true or false.

		True	False
▶	Driver 1 has lost his helmet.	☑	☐
▶	Car 2 has got stuck in the mud.	☐	☑
1	Driver 3 has fallen out.	☐	☐
2	Car 7 has lost its steering wheel.	☐	☐
3	Cars 1 and 3 have crashed.	☐	☐
4	Car 1 has lost a wheel.	☐	☐
5	Driver 1 has fallen into the water.	☐	☐
6	Car 7 has got stuck in the mud.	☐	☐
7	Driver 4 has driven into a tree.	☐	☐
8	Car 3 has a flat tyre.	☐	☐
9	Car 1 has overturned.	☐	☐
10	Car 4 has won.	☐	☐

b Work with a partner.
Ask and answer four questions about the race.

▶ YOU   *Has driver 1 got stuck in the mud?*
    PARTNER   *No, he hasn't.*
▶ YOU   *Which cars have lost wheels?*
    PARTNER   *Cars 1 and 7 have lost wheels.*

3 Activities

a Write new sentences using the present continuous with **for**.

▶ Jane takes tennis lessons. She started in 1991.
Jane has been taking tennis lessons for ... years.

1 Jenny plays the piano. She started in 1988.

2 Tom collects football posters. He started in 1987.

3 Nick goes to a youth club. He started in 1990.

4 Paul draws cartoons. He started in 1989.

5 Jane collects old bottles. She started in 1988.

6 Tom plays football for the school team. He started in 1989.

7 Pam takes riding lessons. She started in 199

8 Ben makes model cars. He started in 1991.

9 Marion writes to a pen-friend in Athens. Sh started in 1989.

10 Peter works in a supermarket on Saturdays. He started in 1992.

11 Jill goes to karate lessons. She started in 198

12 Ann writes poems. She started in 1990.

b Say the answers to (**a**) with **since**.

▶ Jane takes tennis lessons. She started in 199
Jane has been taking tennis lessons since 1991.

---

4 I have been collecting . . .

On a piece of paper, write a sentence about a hobby or sport that you do regularly. Use the present perfect continuous with **for** or **since** to say how long you have been doing it.

I have been collecting ketchup labels for two years.

The teacher will collect all the papers and give them to different students.

Take turns to guess whose paper you have got. Continue until you have found the right person.

▶ YOU *George. Have you been collecting ketchup labels for two years?*

GEORGE *Yes, I have.* OR *No, I haven't.*

Do not write your name on the paper.

5 What have they been doing?

a Complete the sentences with the present perfect simple
or the present perfect continuous.

▶ Jane *has been writing* _____ (write) a letter to a
magazine. She hasn't finished it yet.

1 Ben _____ (look) for his pen-knife,
but he hasn't found it yet.

2 Jenny _____ (wait) for the bus for half
an hour, but it hasn't arrived yet.

3 Nick _____ (play) a computer game
for two hours and he's still playing.

4 Mike hasn't finished painting his car yet. He
_____ (work) on it for two weeks.

5 Amanda _____ (not come) home yet.
She has been shopping in town since 10 o'clock.

6 Mike's car _____ (make) strange
noises. Nick and Jane have cleaned all the parts.

7 Ben has been drawing cartoons for two hours. He
_____ (not finished) yet.

8 Amanda has been waiting for Jenny in town. Jenny
_____ (not arrive) yet.

9 Jane has been knitting a pullover. She
_____ (just finish) it.

10 It _____ (rain) all day and it hasn't
stopped yet.

11 Mr Blake has been marking tests all evening but he
_____ (not find) a perfect one yet.

12 Trig _____ (practise) the present
perfect, but he hasn't got it right.

I have got it right!

I've been practising the present perfect all day...

b Think of a job or activity that you have started but have
not finished, for example, something that you are
making, reading or drawing. Write a short paragraph
about it. Say how long you have been doing it.

4 Have you seen Ben? Present perfect simple or past simple?

NICK	**Have** you **seen** Ben?
TOM	Yes, I **saw** him about ten minutes ago.
NICK	Where **did** you **see** him?
TOM	In the park. He was arguing with Jason.
NICK	Jason? But he's twice as big as Ben. **Have** you ever **had** an argument with him?
TOM	I once **had** a fight with him and two other boys.
NICK	**Did** you **win**?
TOM	No, I **lost**. But it **wasn't** a fair fight.

Later . . .

NICK	Ben! Are you all right? What**'s happened**? You**'ve torn** your trousers, and you**'ve lost** all your buttons.
BEN	Well, I**'ve** only **lost** a few buttons, but Jason **has lost** the fight.

Grammar lesson

Present perfect simple

We use the present perfect simple for a finished action at an unknown or unstated time.

▶ *Have you seen Ben?*
You have torn your trousers.

We use the present perfect simple with **ever**, **never**, **just**, and **not yet**.

▶ *Have you ever had an argument with him?*

Past simple

We use the past simple for an action that started and finished in the past, often with a time expression: **ago**, **last week**, **yesterday** etc.

▶ *I saw him about ten minutes ago.*
I once had a fight with him.
Did you win?

1 This week in Merton

Use the words provided to write one sentence in the present perfect and one sentence in the simple past about each picture.

▶ Mr Curtis broke his nose Saturday
Mr Curtis has broken his nose.
Mr Curtis broke his nose on Saturday.

1 The milkman have accident Monday

_____

_____

2 Miss Pim lost her cat Thursday

_____

3 Sam marry Joan Saturday

_____

4 A thief steal Sue's bag Monday

_____

5 A new restaurant open yesterday

_____

6 Jimmy win the lottery Friday

_____

2 I haven't written for a long time . . .

Complete the letter with the present perfect simple or
the past simple of the verbs in brackets.

Dear Jenny,

  I'm sorry I ► *haven't written* _____ (not write) for a
long time.

  I ► *got* _____ (get) your last letter in
July. A lot of things 1 _____ (happen)
since then.

  In August we 2 _____ (go) on holiday
to Spain. It was great! I 3 _____ (never
have) such a good time. I 4 _____ (even
learn) a few words of Spanish.

  Only two bad things 5 _____ (happen)
there. I 6 _____ (lose) my new camera,
and my sister 7 _____ (fall) off our
hotel balcony and 8 _____ (land) in a
palm tree. She almost 9 _____ (destroy)
the poor tree. I 10 _____ (send) you a
postcard from Granada. 11 _____ (you get)
it?

  In September I 12 _____ (start) at my
new school. I 13 _____ (already make) a
lot of new friends.

  One more bit of news: I 14 _____
(paint) my room – bright orange! Mum and Dad aren't
too happy, but my friends think it's great.

  Please write soon.
  Much love, *Sandra*

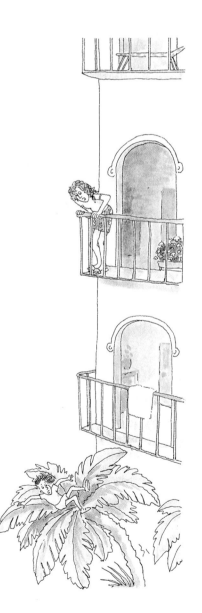

3 Have you seen the film?

Cross out the wrong verb forms.

Yesterday Nick ► met/~~has met~~ Paul and Ben on his way to school.

'*Metal Man Strikes Back* is on at the cinema. 1 Have you seen/Did you see

it?' 2 has asked/asked Nick.

'No. I 3 haven't gone/didn't go to the cinema for months,'

4 answered/has answered Paul. 'I 5 haven't been/wasn't since my

birthday.'

'But I 6 saw/have seen *Metal Man Strikes Back II* and *The Fly's Revenge*,'

7 said/has said Ben. 'I 8 have seen/saw them last week in Bristol. My

cousin's friend 9 has given/gave us two special passes. We saw eight films

in two days,' 10 has explained/explained Ben. 'But I can't remember

any of them.'

4 Have you ever . . . ?

Practise making dialogues with your partner by using
the information in the table. Then fill in the empty
part of the table with your own ideas and make new
dialogues with your partner.

► YOU   *Have you ever been to Spain?*
PARTNER   *Yes, I have.*
YOU   *When did you go there?*
PARTNER   *I went there two years ago.*

Action	What/Where	When	What/Where	When
go	to Spain	two years ago		
see	the Tower of London	in 1991		
watch	the Cosby Show	last night		
read	Frankenstein	two months ago		
hear	a radio play	last week		

5 Daring Dirk, the stunt man

Nick is talking to Daring Dirk, the stunt man. Complete the sentences with the present perfect simple or the past simple of the verbs in brackets.

NICK   Dirk, how long ► *have you been* _____ (you be) a

stunt man?

DIRK   For about ten years now.

NICK   And how ► *did you become* _____ (you become) a

stuntman in the first place?

DIRK   Well, that's a long story. One night about ten years ago

I [1] _____ (stop) a fight in a bar. Jake,

who is now my boss, [2] _____ (see) me in

action and [3] _____ (offer) me a job with

his stunt team. I [4] _____ (take) it.

NICK   [5] _____ (you ever jump) from a

plane?

DIRK   Yes, lots of times. Hanging upside down from a plane is

nothing special.

NICK   [6] _____ (you ever have) a serious

accident?

DIRK   Yes.

NICK   When [7] _____ (it happen) and what

[8] _____ (happen)?

DIRK   Four years ago, I [9] _____ (jump) off a

building onto a trampoline. I [10] _____ (miss)

the trampoline. I [11] _____ (break)

my nose, both arms and both legs.

NICK   What's the most dangerous stunt that you

[12] _____ (ever do)?

DIRK   I think it [13] _____ (be) last year.

I [14] _____ (drive) a car over the edge of

the Grand Canyon.

NICK   [15] _____ (you ever be) married?

DIRK   Only once. My wife [16] _____ (leave) me

after only three months. She couldn't stand the excitement.

5 How much do you want?

NICK   **Can** you lend me some money until the weekend?

TOM   **Have** you spent your pocket money already? **How much do** you want?

NICK   **How much have** you got?

TOM   Not much. **Do** you **need** more than a pound?

NICK   **Haven't** you got more than that?

TOM   No. Sorry. I had to buy a new light for my bike yesterday. **Why don't** you ask someone else?

NICK   **Why did** you need a new light? **What happened**?

TOM   Someone knocked my bike over and broke the front light.

NICK   **Who knocked** it over? **Why didn't** they pay for it?

TOM   I don't know. I didn't see who did it.

Questions

Grammar lesson

Questions

1   In yes/no questions the auxiliary verb comes first. The subject comes next, then the verb.

Can	you	lend me money?	Yes/No.
Have	you	spent it already?	Yes/No.
Do	you	need a pound?	Yes/No.

2   Questions which ask for information begin with question words: **where, when, what, who, which, why, whose, how, how much** etc. We put the question word before the auxiliary verb.

How much	**have**	you got?
Why	**did**	you need it?

3   If **who** or **what** is the subject, the verb in the question is the same as it would be in an affirmative sentence.
   ▶ *Who knocked it over?* (**Who** is the subject.)
   What happened? (**What** is the subject.)

   If **who** or **what** is the object of the verb, we make the question with a form of **do**. Compare:
   ▶ *Who saw Nick?*
   (**Who** is the subject.)
   Who did Nick see?
   (**Nick** is the subject.
   Who is the object.)

4   To make a negative question we add **n't** to the auxiliary verb. Negative questions can express surprise or regret.
   ▶ *Haven't you got more than that?*
   Why didn't they pay for it?

   With **Why don't you/we . . . ?** we can make suggestions.
   ▶ *Why don't you ask someone else?*

1 What kind of person are you?

Complete the questions with the correct form of **be**, **have** or **do**. Then ask your partner the questions and put a √ in the correct box.

			yes	no
▶	*Are*	you sometimes shy?	☐	☑
▶	*Do*	you enjoy puzzles?	☑	☐
1	_____	you sometimes day-dream?	☐	☐
2	_____	you ambitious?	☐	☐
3	_____	your room usually tidy?	☐	☐
4	_____	you like getting up early in the morning?	☐	☐
5	_____	clothes important to you?	☐	☐
6	_____	you serious about sports?	☐	☐
7	_____	being fit important to you?	☐	☐
8	_____	you worry when you make mistakes?	☐	☐
9	_____	you often bored?	☐	☐
10	_____	you cry during sad films?	☐	☐
11	_____	you laugh a lot?	☐	☐
12	_____	you ever written a poem?	☐	☐
13	_____	you ever get angry?	☐	☐
14	_____	some colours make you feel happy?	☐	☐
15	_____	you got a lot of hobbies and interests?	☐	☐

---

2 Who did it?

Last Saturday night someone shot the actor Henry Farthing at his flat in London. Inspector Soames wants to know the answers to these questions.

Put in the correct question words: **who, what, when, where, why, how,** or **how much.** Sometimes two answers are possible.

▶ *Who* _____ shot the actor?

▶ *How much* _____ have the police found out?

1 _____ was the motive?

2 _____ is the main suspect?

3 _____ information have the police got?

4 _____ happened on the night of the murder?

5 _____ did Farthing go when he left the house?

6 _____ did he meet?

7 _____ did he meet him at six o'clock?

8 _____ saw Farthing last?

9 _____ did the murderer get into Farthing's flat?

10 _____ does Janet Jones, his girlfriend, know?

11 _____ did Farthing phone her that evening?

12 _____ is the gun?

3 All about sharks

Use the words in brackets to make questions about sharks.

▶ There are more than 250 types of shark. (How many)

How many types of shark are there?

▶ Sharks live in oceans, but some live in lakes and rivers. (Where)

Where do sharks live?

1 Sharks eat fish, seals, crabs and sea birds – and sometimes surfboards. (What)

2 The Whale Shark is the largest shark. (Which)

3 Sharks' teeth can be 7.5 centimetres long. (How long)

4 Sharks can have 3,000 teeth. (How many)

5 Sharks find their prey with their sense of smell. (How)

6 The Megamouth shark was discovered in 1983. (When)

7 Millions of sharks are killed worldwide every year. (How many)

8 Soup can be made from sharks. (What)

9 In Florida about 120,000 sharks are killed every year. (How many)

10 Fewer than 100 people are attacked by sharks every year. (How many)

Are there any sharks in Merton Pond?

4 Mystery man

Read the mystery man's answers and write the questions. Then guess who it is.

▶ *When were you born?*

I was born in 1947.

1 _____

I was born in the States.

2 _____
_____

I first used a movie camera when I was a boy.

3 _____

I filmed toy trains.

4 _____

I started directing TV programmes when I was 21.

5 _____

I made *Jaws* in 1975.

6 _____

E.T. was my biggest success.

7 _____

It made more than 700 million dollars.

8 _____
_____

I have also directed *Indiana Jones, The Color Purple* and *Hook.*

The mystery man's name is

_____ .

5 Who? What? When?

a Make three quiz questions about each fact. Begin with **who**, **what** or **when**.

▶ William Herschel discovered the planet Uranus in 1781.
Who discovered Uranus?
When did Herschel discover Uranus?
What did Herschel discover in 1781?
When was Uranus discovered?

1 Edison invented the light bulb in 1879.
2 Howard Carter discovered the tomb of Tutankhamun in 1922.
3 Henry Dunant founded the Red Cross in 1864.
4 Daniel Defoe wrote *Robinson Crusoe* in 1719.

b Make quiz questions about the history of your country. Write five questions with **who, when, where, what** or **how**. Ask your questions round the class.

▶ *Where was the first government?*
1 _____
2 _____
3 _____
4 _____
5 _____

6 Suggestions

With a partner, make suggestions with **Why don't you . . . ?**

▶ It's hot in here.
YOU   *It's hot in here.*
PARTNER *Why don't you open a window?*

1 I'm thirsty.
2 I've got a headache.
3 I'm tired.
4 I've got a lot of homework to do.
5 I'm hungry.
6 My bicycle is dirty.
7 My feet are wet.
8 I'm cold.
9 I'm always short of money.
10 My watch is broken.

6 He's good at drawing   **ing** form; **so/neither do I** etc.

TOM   I have an idea. We all need money, so how **about writing** and **selling** a newspaper?

JENNY   That's a good idea, Tom. But is anybody interested **in writing** articles?

JANE   Well, I **like writing** stories. **So does** Ann.

AMANDA   **So do I**. And I **enjoy making up** quizzes and puzzles.

TOM   I **don't mind interviewing** people.

NICK   **Neither do I**.

JENNY   How **about asking** Paul to do the drawings? He's good **at drawing** cartoons.

NICK   **So am I**.

TOM   No, you're not. You can't draw anything.

NICK   **Neither can you**. Anyway, I'd like to write **about cleaning up** the environment. Everybody's interested in that.

Grammar lesson

ing form

We use an **ing** form

1   after the verbs **like, love, enjoy, dislike, hate, can't help, don't mind, start, finish**:
▶   *I like writing stories.*
     I enjoy making up quizzes.
     I don't mind interviewing people.

2   after prepositions **about, at, in** etc.:
▶   *How about asking Paul to do the drawings?*
     He's very good at drawing cartoons.
     Who's interested in writing articles?

so/neither do I etc.

We use **so** . . . to agree with affirmative statements and **neither** . . . to agree with negative statements.

If **be, have, do, can, could, should, will, must** etc. are used in the original statement, we use a form of the same verb after **so** or **neither**.
▶   *Paul is good at drawing cartoons.*
     So am I. So are Tom and Mike.

     You can't draw.
     Neither can you.

But if the verb in the statement is an ordinary verb (**like, enjoy, know** etc.), we use a form of **do** after **so** and **neither**.
▶   *I like writing poems.*
     So does Ann. So do I.

     I don't mind interviewing people.
     Neither do I. Neither does Tom.

Writing for the newspaper

Put the verbs in brackets in the **ing** form.

NICK   People are tired of ▶ *reading* (read) about the same old things in newspapers.

JENNY Have you got any new ideas?

NICK   Well, I'm good at 1_____ (write) about football.

JENNY That's not new! Can't you think of 2_____ (do) anything else?

NICK   Why? Isn't everybody crazy about 3_____ (play) football?

JENNY No. How about 4_____ (have) a music page? You're fond of 5_____ (listen) to music.

NICK   And we could have a joke column. I'm good at 6_____ (tell) jokes.

JENNY Are you still interested in 7_____ (do) an article about the environment?

NICK   Of course. And I've got an idea. How about 8_____ (organize) a competition? Readers have to suggest ways of 9_____ (make) schools 'greener'. They should send in ideas on 10_____ (reduce) waste paper like stopping exams, tests, essays . . .

2 Are you good at drawing?

Write true answers to the questions with verbs in the **ing** form.

▶ Are you good at drawing cartoons?
No, I'm not. But I am good at making model cars.   OR
Yes, I am. I'm also good at painting pictures.

1 Are you good at repairing things?

_____

_____

2 Are you interested in collecting stamps?

_____

_____

3 Are you bored with watching television?

_____

_____

4 Are you good at saving money?

_____

_____

5 Are you interested in reading computer magazines?

_____

_____

6 Are you tired of doing English exercises?

_____

_____

> I'm tired of making mistakes.

3 He loves playing chess

How good a judge of character are you? Look at the three people and say five sentences about each of them with words from each box. Use the **ing** form.

▶ *Miss May dislikes taking exercise.*

like
love
hate
dislike
not mind
enjoy

wash up	drive fast cars
play football	read about philosophy
sew	play chess
take exercise	fix the car
sleep late	listen to music
eat pizza	

MISS MAY   LARRY   PROFESSOR PERKS

4 What Ben can do

Ben has written sentences about himself. Max and Ann have put a ✓ to show that the same is true for them or a × to show that it isn't true for them.

Make sentences about Ben and his friends with **neither** or **so**, like this:

BEN	MAX	ANN
▶ I like basketball.	×	✓
Ben likes basketball. So does Ann.		
▶ I can't speak Greek.	✓	✓
Ben can't speak Greek. Neither can Max or Ann.		
1 I like reading joke books.	✓	×
2 I can stand on my head.	×	✓
3 I am not good at running.	✓	✓
4 I can't play the drums.	×	✓
5 I have got a pet.	✓	✓
6 I don't like country music.	✓	×
7 I have been to Spain.	✓	×
8 I am not shy.	✓	×
9 I don't watch romantic films.	×	✓
10 I don't know how to dance.	×	✓

5 Compare yourself with others

Say six sets of sentences about what you have in common with other people (looks, interests, lik dislikes etc.). Include sentences with **so . . .** or **neither . . .**

▶ *My sister's tall. So am I.* OR
   My brother collects insects. So do I. OR
   My cousin doesn't like mushrooms. Neither do I.

1 My brother/sister/cousin
2 My father
3 My mother
4 My best friend
5 The pupil next to me
6 Our teacher

Amanda doesn't like mice. Neither do I.

6 Match the speakers

Match the statements to the answers.
Who is speaking to whom?

► *Jill is speaking to Jane.*

► JILL   I would like to have a new bicycle.   PETER   So have I.

1 JENNY   I like pizza.   JANE   So would I.

2 SAM   I won't be fourteen until next year.   TRIG   So do I.

3 PAUL   I don't like going to the dentist's.   BRIAN   Neither will I.

4 AMANDA I can't dance very well.   MARION   Neither could I.

5 NICK   I have bought a new cassette.   TOM   So am I.

6 BEN   I couldn't do the Maths test.   JAMES   Neither can I.

 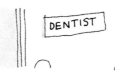

7 DAVE   I'm going to the pop   SIMON   Neither do I.
               concert tomorrow.

7 Could you help us?

would, could for requests;
Uncountable nouns

NICK   Mike, have you heard about our newspaper?

MIKE   Yes, I have. It sounds like a great idea. But I expect you'll need **some help**.

NICK   Well, we need **some advice** and **a lot of information**. **Would you** help us with a few things?

MIKE   Of course. What can I do?

NICK   **Could you** drive us to interviews? And **could** I borrow your microphone and tape recorder?

... and could you lend us some money for a computer. And could I use ...

Grammar lesson

would, could

When you ask for something, **would** and **could** are more polite than **can**. We use **would you** or **could you** when we ask someone to do something.

▶ *Could you drive us to interviews?*

We use **could I** and **could we** to ask for permission.

▶ *Could I borrow your microphone?*

Uncountable nouns

We can count nouns like **book**. They have a singular and a plural form.

Some nouns are uncountable. They have no plural form and they take a singular verb. We use them alone or with **some/any**, **a lot of**, **not much**, **how much**. We do not use them with **a/an** or with numbers.

Kinds of food, materials (e.g. **sand**, **gold**, **wood**) and abstract nouns are often uncountable. Here are some more examples:

advice	jewellery	news
fun	knowledge	progress
furniture	luggage	traffic
help	money	work
information	music	

▶ *We need **some advice** and **a lot of information**.*

With **a piece of** we can make uncountable nouns countable: **a piece of advice**, **two pieces of news**.

The word **hair** is countable and uncountable.

A single hair is countable.

▶ *There are **two hairs** in my soup.*

The hair on your head is uncountable.

▶ *My **hair** is too long.*

1 Would you change the oil, please?

Mike has taken his car to the garage.
Here is his list of jobs for the mechanic.
What does he say? Begin with **Would you . . . ?**

▶ change the oil
Would you change the oil, please?

1 check the brakes

_____

2 oil the doors

_____

3 replace the broken light

_____

4 check the tyres

_____

5 repair the radio

_____

6 put in a new battery

_____

Would you send the bill to my mother, please?

2 Being polite

Make requests with **Could I . . . ?**

▶ You are in a shoe shop. You want to try on the black shoes in the shop window.
Could I try on the black shoes in the window, please?

1 You are in a café. Ask for the bill.

_____

2 You are at an airport check-in desk. You would like to have a window seat.

_____

3 You are sitting in a restaurant. Ask someone at another table for the salt.

_____

4 You are having a meal at a friend's house. You would like some more potatoes.

_____

5 You are in your English class. You want to borrow your teacher's dictionary.

_____

6 You are in a restaurant. You would like to use the telephone.

_____

3 The Ancient Egyptians

a Do you know these facts about the Ancient Egyptians?
Cross out the wrong words.

We have found a lot of interesting | ▶ information/~~informations~~ |

about life in Ancient Egypt.

Most Egyptian children went to school when they were eight.

There was sport for the boys only, which wasn't | ▶ a/much |

fun for the girls. The teachers were very strict, but the Egyptians

liked | 1 musics/music | and most children learned to play an

instrument.

Egyptian houses did not have as | 2 much/many | furniture as our

houses. The furniture | 3 was/were | usually made of | 4 –/a |

wood, but rich people had furniture decorated with | 5 an/– |

ivory or gold.

Their clothes were made of linen but in winter, some people wore

| 6 a/– | wool. Because of the heat, most people wore their

| 7 hair/hairs | short. Rich people sometimes wore wigs.

Women wore | 8 –/a | beautiful jewellery. Egypt had gold mines,

so | 9 a lot of/many | jewellery was made of | 10 –/a | gold. All

men and women, whether rich or poor, wore make-up and perfume.

They got milk and | 11 meat/meats | from goats, and they ate a

lot of | 12 fish/fishes |. They sweetened their | 13 food/foods |

with honey. They baked their | 14 bread/breads | in mud-brick

ovens. They also ate | 15 a lot of/many | fruit.

b Say if the sentences are true or false. Correct the false ones.

▶ The Ancient Egyptians had a lot of furniture in their houses.
False. They didn't have much furniture in their houses.

▶ They didn't wear their hair long.
True.

1 We haven't found much information about life in Ancient Egypt.
2 Not much Egyptian jewellery was made of gold.
3 They didn't eat much fruit.
4 They ate a lot of fish.
5 The men wore make-up and perfume.
6 The children had a lot of fun at school.

c Work with a partner. Ask and answer four questions about the Ancient Egyptians.
Ask about their furniture, their clothes, their jewellery, their hair or their food.

▶ YOU   *Did the Ancient Egyptians wear their hair long?*

PARTNER   *No, they wore their hair short.*

---

4 Find the mystery word

Which words are uncountable?
Ring the uncountable words and fit them into the puzzle (across) in order to find the mystery word (down).

suitcase	gold	furniture
coin	fact	money
progress	luggage	story
music	news	(fun)
answer	chair	knowledge
week	sandwich	song

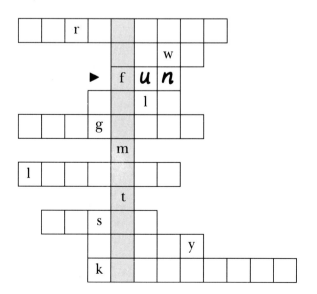

The mystery word is: _____

8 She lets Ben do anything

JENNY   What's wrong, Jane? You look upset.

JANE   I want to go sailing, but my aunt **won't let** me **go**. She's too strict. She **lets** Ben **do** everything, and he's younger than me. Yesterday she **let** him **watch** TV until midnight. She **makes** me **do** the washing up every day, but she never **makes** Ben **do** anything. It isn't fair.

Later, Jenny tells Nick about Jane's problem.

JENNY   Jane **says** that she **wants** to go sailing, but her aunt **won't let** her go. She **says** her aunt **makes** her do the washing up every day but she never **makes** Ben do anything.

NICK   It's exactly the same at our house. Mum **makes** me **tidy** up and she never **lets** me **play** loud music.

Grammar lesson

let, make

After **let** and **make** we use an object + infinitive without **to**.

| She | lets | him | do | everything. |
| She | makes | me | do | the washing up. |

Indirect speech (present)

This is direct speech.
▶ Jane says to Jenny: *'I want to go sailing.'*

This is indirect (reported) speech.
We can leave out **that**.
▶ *Jane says (that) she wants to go sailing.*

say is a reporting verb. If the reporting verb is in the present tense, there is no change of tense in indirect speech.
▶ *'I want to go sailing.'* (present direct)
   *She **says** she **wants** to go sailing.*
   (present indirect)

Sometimes other words change in indirect speech, for example, pronouns.
▶ Jane says, *'My aunt won't let me go.'* (direct)
   *Jane says that **her** aunt won't let **her** go.*
   (indirect)

1 It makes me laugh

What do these things make you or others do?
Use words from each list to make ten sentences.

▶ *Onions make my sister cry.*
Onions don't make me cry.

onions			
puzzles			feel happy
jokes			laugh
presents		you	cry
toothache	make(s)	me	feel cross
quizzes	doesn't/don't make	my sister/brother	think
a new hair style		my friend	feel tired
funny cartoons		some people	feel good
exercise			
sad films			

2 They let me have parties

a Say four things from the box that your parents **let** you do. Say four things that they **don't let** you do.

▶ *They let me have parties.*
They don't let me stay out late.

have parties
stay out late
go on holiday with friends
buy your own clothes
go out in the evenings alone
bring friends home
listen to loud music
wear whatever clothes you want
watch late films on TV
talk on the telephone for hours
spend lots of money on records

b What do your parents **make** you do?
What **don't** they **make** you do?
Write a short paragraph.

Here are some ideas:

keep all your things in your room
help at home
eat everything on your plate
get up early on Sundays
do homework every night
do the washing up
clean your shoes

3 Kidnapped!

Someone has kidnapped the son of the industrialist James Thornton. The Thorntons have just received this note from the kidnappers.

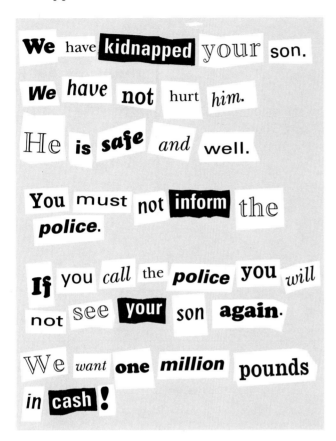

We have **kidnapped** your son.

We have **not** hurt *him*.

He **is safe** *and* well.

You must not **inform** the **police**.

If you *call* the **police** you *will* not see **your** son **again**.

We *want* **one million** pounds in **cash** !

What does the note say? Finish telling what the note says.

▶ *The note says that they have kidnapped the Thorntons' son. It says . . .*

4 Sports at school

Amanda is doing a survey for the newspaper. She is asking pupils what they think about sports at school.

I hate running round the gym and getting hot and sweaty. We shouldn't have to do games at school. It's got nothing to do with learning.

JILL

Everybody should do sports every day. Two lessons a week are not enough. Most pupils don't take physical fitness seriously enough.

SIMON

They should teach judo or tennis, not just running or jumping. I would like to do aerobics and self-defence.

BETH

I am very good at games. I love all sports: swimming, skiing, football . . . It's too bad we have to learn maths and geography at school.

MARK

I like sports but I don't like the ones we do at school. I once fell off the rope and broke my thumb.

DAVE

Teachers shouldn't give marks for games. Some pupils are too weak or unfit. It isn't their fault if they're not good.

MARIA

a Answer the questions.

▶ What does Simon say about the number of sports lessons?

He says that two lessons a week are not enough.

1 What does Beth say about judo and tennis?

_____

_____

2 What does Dave say about the sports they do at school?

_____

_____

3 What does Maria say about marks for games?

_____

_____

4 What does Simon say about physical fitness?

_____

_____

5 What does Mark say about maths and geography?

_____

_____

6 What does Jill say about running round the gym?

_____

_____

7 What does Dave say about a sports injury?

_____

_____

8 What does Jill say about games at school?

_____

_____

9 What does Maria say about pupils who are too weak or unfit?

_____

_____

10 What does Beth say about aerobics and self-defence?

_____

_____

b Work with a partner. Say what you think about the number of times you have games classes each week and the kinds of games you play.

Your partner then reports what you say to the class.

▶ YOU   *We have too many games classes.*
PARTNER   *John says we have too many games classes.*

5 Headlines

Make up three news headlines. They can be serious, amazing or funny. They don't have to be true. Write them on a piece of paper.

Your teacher will collect them and give them to other pupils. They must tell the class what the headlines say.

▶ *It says that aliens have invaded New York.*

Aliens have invaded New York.

9 The film had almost finished

**Past perfect simple;
Past perfect continuous**

TOM Did you enjoy the film yesterday?

NICK Well, it's a long story. I got on the bus but I **had forgotten** my bus fare.

TOM So what did you do?

NICK I got off the bus and ran home, but everybody **had gone** out. I couldn't get in, because I **hadn't taken** my key. So I went to Paul's house to borrow some money . . .

TOM Wait, let me guess: **he'd spent** all his money that afternoon.

NICK No. He **hadn't come** home yet. When he finally arrived, I **had been waiting** for twenty minutes. After he **had lent** me some money, I caught the next bus. But when I got to the cinema, the film **had** almost **finished**.

Grammar lesson

Past perfect simple

1 We form the past perfect simple with **had** + past participle. Look at the list of irregular past participles at the back of the book.
   ▶ *I **had forgotten** my money.*
      *Nick **hadn't put** his key in his pocket.*
      ***Had** you **forgotten** your key?*

Long forms	Short forms
I **had** forgotten	**I'd** forgotten
I **had not** put	I **hadn't** put

2 We use the past perfect for a past action which happened before another past action.

Yesterday morning	Yesterday evening	Now
*I **had forgotten** my money.*	*I couldn't buy a ticket.*	*Nick is telling Tom his story.*

This happened before that.

3 We often use the past perfect with **because** and **after**.
   ▶ *I couldn't buy a ticket because I **had forgotten** my money.*
      *After Paul **had lent** me some money, I caught the next bus.*

Past perfect continuous

We form the past perfect continuous with **had been** + an **ing** form for all persons.

▶ *I had been waiting*.

We use the past perfect continuous for a past action which continued until another past action happened.

Past	Past	Now
Nick **had been waiting** . . . (*for twenty minutes*).	*Paul arrived*.	*Nick is telling Tom what happened.*

This happened before that.

1 Mystery word

Can you recognize the past perfect forms?
If the verb is in the past perfect simple or continuous form, leave the letter in the box at the end of the sentence. If the verb is in another form, cross out the letter in the box. If your answers are correct, you can answer the question below.

▶	I had seen him before.	H
▶	Has she written to you?	X̶
1	I am talking on the phone.	U
2	The boy hadn't been to the disco.	A
3	She had long hair.	N
4	Had she forgotten to pay?	N
5	Your friends have arrived.	A
6	How long had he been waiting?	N
7	We had had supper.	I
8	Had you met him before?	B
9	He hasn't been living here long.	A
10	She hadn't had a shower.	A
11	Had she been writing a letter?	L

Question: Who crossed the Alps with thirty-seven elephants in 281 BC?

Answer: _H_____

2 What came first?

Read the sentences and put a ring round the action
that came first. Then write one sentence with the
past perfect simple and **because**.

▶ Nick (forgot) his key. He couldn't get in.
  Nick couldn't get in because he had forgotten his key.

▶ Jane went to the police station. Someone (stole) her bike.
  Jane went to the police station because someone had stolen her bike.

1 Tom spent all his pocket money. He couldn't buy a pen.

   _____

2 Ben felt ill. He ate four packets of crisps.

   _____

3 Jenny didn't have breakfast. She felt very hungry.

   _____

4 Mr Bell couldn't read his letters. He broke his glasses.

   _____

5 Nick couldn't play basketball. He hurt his thumb.

   _____

6 Ben didn't turn off the tap. The bath overflowed.

   _____

7 Mike forgot his wallet. He couldn't pay the restaurant bill.

   _____

8 Jenny got sunburned. She forgot to put on some sun cream.

   _____

9 Jane couldn't go out. She didn't do her homework.

   _____

10 Sue failed the test. She didn't revise for it.

   _____

3 Harry's career

Read the notes about Harry's career then answer the questions with **after** and the past perfect simple.

▶ When did he join the army?
He joined the army after he had left school.

1 When did he rob the bank?

_____

2 When did he work as a waiter?

_____

3 When did he get a job as a singer?

_____

4 Did he form the pop group before or after he had made a record?

_____

5 When did he become a millionaire?

_____

6 Did he write his book before or after he had become a millionaire?

_____

7 When did he go to live in Los Angeles?

_____

8 When did the pop group break up?

_____

9 When did he marry Goldie?

_____

10 Did he make the film before or after he had bought the restaurants?

_____

Harry Biggs

left school
↓
joined the army
↓
got a job in a London bank
↓
lost his job
↓
robbed a bank
↓
went to prison
↓
worked as a waiter
↓
got a job as a singer in a night club
↓
made a record
↓
formed a pop group
↓
became a millionaire
↓
wrote a book
↓
went to live in Los Angeles
↓
pop group broke up
↓
married Goldie Bruce, film star
↓
bought a chain of restaurants
↓
made a film

4 Who's guilty?

Inspector Soames is investigating the murder of Henry Farthing. He has discovered that shots were heard at 9.13 last Saturday night. He has asked everyone in Henry Farthing's block of flats what they had been doing before they heard the shot.

Look at the picture and write what they said they had been doing.

▶ THE PARKERS *We had been having our supper.*

▶ BILL JONES *My wife and I had been watching television.*

1 THE WILSONS _____

_____

2 MARY WELLS _____

_____

3 THE COOKS _____

_____

4 THE BAXTERS _____

_____

5 MAX PIM _____

_____

6 THE WOODS _____

_____

7 SARAH GREEN _____

_____

8 ALF BROWN _____

_____

Do you know who the murderer was? Write your reason.

I think the murderer was _____

because he/she said that he/she _____ ,

but he/she _____ .

Henry Farthing

The Parkers

Mrs Jones

The Wilsons

Mary Wells

The Cooks

The Baxters

Max Pim

The Woods

Sarah Green

Alf Brown

5 What had they been doing?

Use the words from the box in the past perfect continuous to complete the sentences.

eat	repair	try	revise
fight	run	wait	swim
read ✓	sit	watch	

▶ Jenny's eyes were tired.
She _had been reading_ all evening.

1 Amanda was hot and sore.
She _____ in the sun.

2 Jane had oil on her hands.
She _____ a friend's motor bike.

3 Tom was hot and out of breath.
He _____ in the park.

4 Ben's clothes were dirty.
He _____ with Jason.

5 Sue was angry. She _____ for Mike for twenty minutes.

6 Jane was nervous.
She _____ a TV programme about crime.

7 Jenny had a stomach ache.
She _____ sour grapes.

8 Sue was tired.
She _____ for exams all night.

9 Mike was cold.
He _____ in an unheated pool.

10 Trig fell asleep.
He _____ to learn the past perfect continuous.

6 About you

Talk about the last time
- you felt very tired
- your feet ached
- you were very wet

What had you been doing? How long had you been doing it?

▶ *Last Thursday evening I felt very tired because I had been playing basketball for two hours.*

▶ *Last night my feet ached because I had been walking around town for hours.*

▶ *Last Sunday I was very wet because I had been standing in the rain in the cinema queue for half an hour.*

10 I've bought you a present

**Verbs with two objects;
Time clauses**

MIKE Happy birthday, Ben! Here's the post. It
came **while** I was making breakfast.
All your friends have **sent you birthday
cards**.

JANE Aunt Sarah has **made a cake for you**.
And she has **bought you a new red
sweater**. She **showed it to me**.

MIKE And this is my present. I got it **when** I
went to town last week. You'll love it. **As
soon as** you have opened it we'll have
breakfast.

BEN Oh thanks . . . It's a bottle of
perfume . . .

MIKE Oh no! It's the wrong box. If I've **given
the perfume to you**, then I've **given the
football socks to Sue**.

Grammar lesson

Verbs with two objects

Some verbs like **give**, **send**, **show** can have two objects:
a direct object and an indirect object. The direct object
tells us what someone gives, shows etc. The indirect
object tells us the person who is given or shown
something. Compare the word order in (**a**) and (**b**).

a	Subject	Verb	Indirect object	Direct object
	Mike	gave	Ben	the perfume.
	Aunt Sarah	showed	Jane	the sweater.

b	Subject	Verb	Direct object	Indirect object
	Mike	gave	the socks	**to** Sue.
	Aunt Sarah	showed	the sweater	**to** Jane.

We use word order (**a**) when the direct object (the thing) is
more important. We use word order (**b**) with **to** when the
indirect object (the person) is more important.

Other verbs with two objects are **offer**, **pass**, **teach**, **write**,
buy, **make**. With **buy** and **make** we use **for** instead of **to**.

▶ *Aunt Sarah has **made you** a cake.* OR
*Aunt Sarah has **made** a cake **for you**.*

Time clauses

Words such as **when**, **while**, **as soon as**, **before**, **after**, **until** can introduce a time clause.

▶ *I got it **when** I went to town.*

When two actions happen at the same time, we use **while** to introduce the longer action.

▶ *The cards came **while** I was making breakfast.*

In time clauses we often use past or perfect tenses, but we don't normally use **will** or **would**.

1 Get the order right

Put the words in order and write correct sentences.

▶ | Mike | | a letter | | sent | | his girlfriend | .

Mike sent his girlfriend a letter.

1 | Jane | | her photos | | to | | showed | | her friends | .

2 | Nick | | an old lady | | his seat | | offered | | to | .

3 | to | | Jenny | | all her friends | | sent | | party invitations | .

4 | me | | Can you | | that video | | pass | ?

5 | a ring | | Did | | Mike | | buy | | Sue | ?

6 | Has | | Nick | | you | | his new joke | | told | ?

7 | Amanda | | Who | | the silver bracelet | | gave | ?

8 | a letter | | Did Tom | | you | | or | | send | | a postcard | ?

9 | Ben | | his new computer game | | to | | showed | | Nick | .

2 Happy birthday!

a Look at the maze and say what they gave their friends for their birthdays.
Put the words in the same order as the example.

▶ *Mike gave Sue the football socks.*

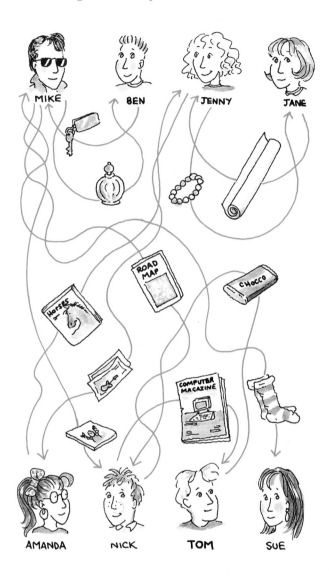

b Answer the questions, like this:
▶ Did Mike give Ben the football socks?
No, he didn't. He gave the football socks to Sue.
1 Did Mike give Sue the perfume?
2 Did Jane give Amanda the bracelet?
3 Did Jenny give Jane the concert tickets?
4 Did Amanda give Jane the book about horses?
5 Did Jenny give Amanda the poster?
6 Did Nick give Tom the road map?
7 Did Nick give Mike the computer magazine?
8 Did Tom give Mike the bar of chocolate?
9 Did Ben give Nick the key ring?
10 Did Mike give Tom the computer game?

3 Mike

Read about Mike and cross out the wrong word.

Mike will finish secondary school next year,

▶ when/~~until~~ he's eighteen. He wants to go to university 1 after/before he has left school. He's very good with computers. He was able to write computer programs 2 when/before he was only twelve.

He can play the drums and the trumpet. He sometimes practises at night 3 when/until everybody is trying to sleep, or early on Sunday mornings 4 before/after anybody gets up. The neighbours are not too happy 5 until/when he plays with all the windows open.

He hasn't got much money, so he would like to have a part-time job 6 while/after he's at university, probably playing in a band. He wants to see the world 7 before/after he gets married, and he doesn't want to get married 8 until/as soon as he is thirty.

He would like to work abroad 9 until/after he has finished his studies. 10 As soon as/While he has passed his exams, he will apply for a job in Australia or New Zealand – as a computer specialist or as a drummer.

4 Young Mozart

Complete the text about Mozart's childhood.
Put in **when**, **while**, **as soon as**, **after** or **before**.
Sometimes, more than one answer is possible.

▶ *When* _____ Wolfgang Amadeus Mozart was
born, his father worked as a violinist at the court at
Salzburg.

Mozart's father was an ambitious man.
1 _____ Mozart was only four, his father
started practising the piano with him.
2 _____ he realized how talented Mozart
and his sister were, he began to teach them all he knew
about music.

3 _____ Mozart was five years old, he
had already learned to play the harpsichord. He
started composing songs 4 _____ he was
only five – 5 _____ he could read or
write. His father used to write down the notes
6 _____ Mozart played his compositions
at the piano.

In 1762, Mozart's father took his children to Munich
and then to Vienna. In Vienna Mozart played for the
Empress Maria Theresa. She loved his playing.
7 _____ he had finished playing, he
climbed on her knee and gave her a kiss.

The following year, the Mozart family went on a tour of
Europe. In Paris he played at the court of Louis xv.
Mozart played the harpsichord 8 _____
one of the king's daughters sang an Italian song. Mozart
had never heard the song before.

9 _____ he had learned to write, he
wrote down his first great piano concertos. In Rome in
1770, 10 _____ Mozart was still only
fourteen, he heard music in the Sistine Chapel.
11 _____ he got home, he wrote the
music down perfectly from memory –
12 _____ he had heard it only once.

11 She said that I was lying

Indirect speech in the past

MRS FOX   There you are! I've finally caught you. You **stole** a Walkman from my shop yesterday.

BEN   I **don't know** anything about a Walkman and I **wasn't** in your shop yesterday.

MRS FOX   You **are lying**. Boys always **tell** lies. I **saw** you running away. You **were wearing** the same blue jacket. I **will call** the police. You'll see!

Later Ben tells Nick what Mrs Fox said.

BEN   Mrs Fox **said** that I **had stolen** a Walkman from her shop. I **told** her that I **didn't know** anything about it and that I **hadn't been** in her shop yesterday.

NICK   That's true. You were with me all day.

BEN   She **said** she **had seen** me running away.

NICK   But why does she think it was you?

BEN   She said I **had been wearing** the same blue jacket. She **said** she **would** tell the police. What shall I do?

Grammar lesson

Indirect speech in the past

When the reporting verb is in the past, (she **said**, I **told** her) the verb tense in direct speech changes when we report it.

Learn these changes:

Direct speech		Indirect speech
present	→	past
past	→	past perfect
present perfect	→	past perfect

Direct speech		Indirect speech
can	→	**could**
will	→	**would**
may	→	**might**

▶ *She said, 'You **are lying**.'* (present)
*She said that I **was lying**.* (past)

▶ *She said, 'You **stole** a Walkman.'* (past)
*She said that I **had stolen** a Walkman.* (past perfect)

▶ *She said, 'I **will** call the police.'* (will)
*She said that she **would** call the police.* (would)

If the direct speech is a general statement, the tense does not always change:

▶ *She said, 'Boys always **tell** lies.'* (present)
*She said that boys always **tell** lies.* (present)

4 It wasn't Ben

Nick wants to help Ben. He wants to find out who stole the Walkman. He asks his friends some questions. Here are their answers.

PETER   Mrs Fox always blames the wrong people.

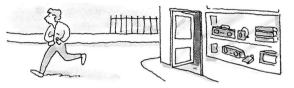

PAUL   I·saw a tall blond boy running out of the shop.

MAX   Lots of boys wear blue jackets.

JILL   I don't know anything about it.

ALICE   Mrs Fox can't see very well.

JAMES   I'll ask the boys in my class about it.

MARY   There were three or four boys in the shop at five o'clock.

TONY   Mrs Fox has told the police.

JANE   Ben has never stolen anything.

AMANDA   Mrs Fox can't prove anything.

TOM   We will all help Ben.

CHRIS   I know who stole it but I won't tell you.

JOAN   I will visit Ben if he goes to prison.

Write what they said.

▶ Peter *said that Mrs Fox always blamed the wrong people.*

1 Paul _____

2 Max _____

3 Jill _____

4 Alice _____

5 James _____

6 Mary _____

7 Tony _____

8 Jane _____

9 Amanda _____

10 Tom _____

11 Chris _____

12 Joan _____

2 You stopped without warning

A van driver and a girl on a motor bike have had an accident. Amanda heard what they said.

GIRL   What a stupid thing to do! You stopped without warning.

DRIVER   I had to stop. A dog ran across the road. But you weren't looking. And now my van's badly damaged.

GIRL   I didn't see a dog. I'll write down your name and insurance number. My light is broken and the bike won't start.

DRIVER   It only needs a bit of paint. It can be fixed in no time. But the back of my van's a mess. The repairs will cost hundreds of pounds.

Later, Amanda tells Nick what she heard. The girl said that the driver

▶ *had stopped* _____ without warning. The driver said that he ^{1}_____ to stop because a dog ^{2}_____ across the road. He said the girl ^{3}_____ and his van ^{4}_____ damaged.

Then the girl said that she ^{5}_____ a dog. She said she ^{6}_____ down the man's name and insurance number. She said her light ^{7}_____ broken and the bike ^{8}_____ start.

The driver said the bike only ^{9}_____ a bit of paint and it ^{10}_____ be fixed in no time. But h van ^{11}_____ a mess and the repair ^{12}_____ cost hundreds of pounds.

3 How 'green' are you?

Nick has written questions for a survey. Ask the questions round the class. Count the number of **Yes** and **No** answers and write the results in the questionnaire.

		Yes	No
▶	Have you ever used a bottle bank?	5	11
1	Do you buy canned drinks?	___	___
2	Do you sometimes drop litter in the street?	___	___
3	Do you use disposable pens?	___	___
4	Did you walk or cycle to school today?	___	___
5	Do you turn off unnecessary lights?	___	___
6	Do you think about noise pollution?	___	___
7	Do you write on both sides of a sheet of paper?	___	___
8	Have you read about the hole in the ozone layer?	___	___
9	Do you use plastic bags more than once?	___	___
10	Do you eat fast food?	___	___

Now take turns to say the results of the survey.
▶ *Five pupils said that they had used a bottle bank.*
Eleven pupils said that they hadn't used a bottle bank.

4 Can TV make you violent?

Tom is doing a survey for the newspaper. He is asking people if TV can make you violent.

DAVE

> TV can't make you violent if you are a calm person. I have seen a few violent films, but I don't take them seriously.

JILL

> Violence can influence young people. If they see too many violent programmes, they will believe that life is like that.

> I don't watch really violent films. The pictures on the news are bad enough.

JENNY

> TV violence can only make you aggressive if you are a weak person. I will never rob a bank just because someone in a film does it.

SIMON

> If you're a nice person, TV violence won't change that. You can always switch off.

MAX

> I saw a violent film last week. I know the blood wasn't real, but a lot of younger children don't know that.

NICK

a What did they say?

▶ Dave said that *TV could not make you violent if you were a calm person.*

1 Dave also said that . . .
2 Jenny said that . . .
3 Max said that . . .
4 Nick said . . .
5 Jill said . . .
6 Simon said . . .

b Work with a partner.
Tell your partner what you think about TV violence. Say two sentences.
Your partner then tells the class what you said.

▶ YOU   *I think that violence on television is bad. I never watch violent films.*

PARTNER   *He said that he thought violence on television was bad. He said that he never watched violent films.*

12 You needn't learn . . . mustn't, needn't; had better, would rather

JENNY Nick, we **had better go** to bed. It's very late.

NICK I know, but **I would rather help** Trig **than** go to bed. He's tearing up his English exercise book and he's throwing his grammar book round the room. I don't think he's very happy.

JENNY Well, you **had better not stay up** too long.

NICK Trig, stop it. You **mustn't throw** your books at the wall. It won't help and you might break something. You **needn't work** at your English now. What are you learning?

TRIG **abbreviation** [n] 1 U abbreviating, being abbreviated 2 C shortened form of a word, phrase, etc: 'Sept' is an abbreviation for 'September' . . .

NICK But Trig, that's from the dictionary. You **needn't learn** the whole dictionary by heart!

Grammar lesson

mustn't, needn't

After **mustn't** and **needn't** we use the infinitive without **to**.

1 We use **mustn't** when we forbid something. It is stronger than **shouldn't**.
▶ *Trig, you **mustn't throw** your books!*

2 We use **needn't** when it is not necessary to do something.
▶ *You **needn't learn** the whole dictionary by heart.*

Instead of **needn't** we can say **don't have to**.
▶ *We **needn't/don't have to** go to school on Sundays.*

had better, would rather

After **had better** and **would rather** we also use the infinitive without **to**.

1 We use **had better** to give advice in a particular situation. For general advice we use **should**.
▶ *You **had better go** to bed now. It's very late.*
*You**'d better not stay** up too late tonight.*

The short form is **'d better** (**not**).

2 We use **would rather** to say what we prefer to do. If we mention two things, we use **than**.
▶ *I **would rather help** Trig **than go** to bed.*

The short form is **'d rather** (**not**).
▶ *I'd rather (not).*

1 Signs

What do the signs say?
Make sentences with **mustn't** or **needn't**.

▶ You *mustn't* fish here.

▶ You *needn't* wash it in hot water.

1 You _____ make a noise between
ten in the evening and seven in the morning.

2 You _____ be a member.

3 You _____ reserve a table.

4 You _____ cycle here.

5 You _____ pay with cash.

6 You _____ serve yourself.

2 Holidays

a   You are going to Jamaica for a beach holiday. You are staying at a hotel. What **mustn't** you forget? What **needn't** you take? Write five sentences.

passport ✓	swimming costume
tin opener	sleeping bag
tent	plane ticket

▶ *You mustn't forget your passport.*

_____

_____

_____

_____

b   Now you are going on a camping holiday near where you live. What **mustn't** you forget? What **needn't** you do/take/pack, etc.? Say five sentences.

▶ *You needn't take your passport.*

3 My dream house

What kind of house would you like to live in one day? Use **mustn't** and **needn't**. Write five sentences.

▶ *It mustn't be too far from a town.*

▶ *It needn't look like Buckingham Palace.*

1 _____

2 _____

3 _____

4 _____

5 _____

4 What had they better do?

Give advice by writing a sentence with **had better** and a sentence with **had better not**.

▶ It's raining. Jenny is going out.
She had better take her umbrella.
She had better not forget her umbrella.

1 Nick wants a drink of milk. The milk smells sour.

2 Jane has a temperature. She wants to go out.

3 Mr Bell is going for a long drive. There isn't much petrol in the car.

4 Amanda and Jenny want to leave school early. They need permission from Miss Mill.

5 Mrs Bell has toothache. She doesn't want to go to the dentist's.

6 Ben is going to watch a horror video. It will scare him.

7 Mr Bell is driving too fast. The speed limit is 30 miles an hour.

8 Aunt Sarah hasn't got any bread. She is having visitors to tea.

9 Nick is playing his music too loudly. Mr Bell is working in his study.

10 Tom and Nick want to go to the cinema. The film starts in ten minutes.

5 Preferences

What would you rather do?
Use **I would rather . . .** to say what you prefer.

▶ buy a CD-player OR save my money
I would rather save my money than buy a CD-player.

1 go to the cinema OR stay at home
2 buy a mountain bike OR save money
3 revise for an English test OR go to a party
4 look round a museum OR watch a basketball match
5 go up in a rocket OR go down in a submarine
6 work as a fashion designer OR be a journalist
7 listen to music at home OR go to a pop concert
8 learn windsurfing OR take a course in parachute jumping
9 live abroad OR stay in my country
10 play football OR watch a football match on television

13 It must be a joke **must**, **can't** for deductions; **so**, **such**

NICK   Jenny, look at this letter. It says 'For the young Bells. Open with care.'
The handwriting is **so strange**. I don't recognize it.

JENNY   Let me have a look. It's **so untidy** that I can hardly read it.

NICK   Well, it **must be** for us. It **can't be** for Mum and Dad. Their names aren't on the envelope.

JENNY   And it **can't be** a bill. I bet it's from Uncle Joe. He's **such** a joker. Let's open it.

NICK   It is from Uncle Joe. He's sent us tickets for a helicopter flight over London! He always has **such** great ideas.

Grammar lesson

must, can't for deductions

If we cannot explain a problem, we can make deductions from the facts. We say what is logical in the situation.

We use **must** to give a logical answer or explanation:

▶ *It **must be** for us.*

For the negative we use **can't**.

▶ *It **can't be** a bill.*

After **must** and **can't** we use the infinitive without **to**.

so, such

1   We use **so** with an adjective alone.
    ▶ *The handwriting is **so strange**.*

2   We use **such** with a noun (with or without an adjective before it).
    ▶ *He always has **such great ideas**.*
        *He's **such** a joker.*

    Compare:
    ▶ *It's **so strange**.*
        *It's **such strange handwriting**.*

3   After **so** and **such** we can use **that** to show result.
    ▶ *It's **so untidy that** I can hardly read it.*
        *It's **such untidy handwriting that** I can hardly read it.*

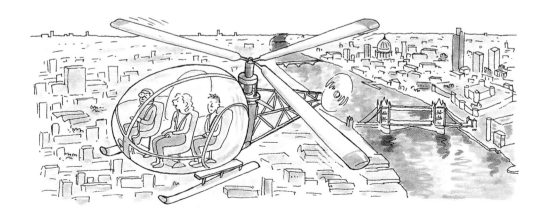

1 Whose luggage is it?

Kathy, Frank and Susan are going on holiday. One of them is going to Spain, one to the French Alps and one to Italy. But who is going where?

a What does the luggage tell you about the owners?
Complete the sentences with **must** or **can't** and **be**,
have or **like**.

▶	The owner	*must be*	able to play tennis.
▶	The owner	*can't be*	a man.
1	The owner	_____	British.
2	The owner	_____	reading detective stories.
3	The owner	_____	going to a sunny country.

4	The owner	_____	a woman.
5	The owner	_____	able to read French.
6	The owner	_____	big feet.
7	The owner	_____	chocolate.
8	The owner	_____	going on a skiing holiday.

9	The owner	_____	a man.
10	The owner	_____	jazz.
11	The owner	_____	long hair.
12	The owner	_____	learning Italian.

b Now solve the puzzle. Write who the luggage must belong to.

1 The suitcase _____

2 The backpack _____

3 The straw bag _____

Write where they must be going.

4 Kathy _____

5 Frank _____

6 Susan _____

2 Which one is it?

Make deductions by reading the clues and completing all the sentences with **can't be** or **must be** as in the example.

▶ **elephant giraffe panda kangaroo lion**

It lives in Africa, so *it can't be a panda or a kangaroo.*

It hasn't got a trunk, so *it can't be an elephant.*

It is much taller than a man, so *it can't be a lion.*

Answer: *It must be a giraffe.*

1 **China   the USA   Italy   Spain   Fiji**

It isn't in Europe, so _____

It's a very big country, so _____

The people speak English, so _____

Answer: _____

2 **Rome   New York   Paris   Chicago   Oxford**

It isn't in America, so _____

The people don't speak French, so _____

It's a capital city, so _____

Answer: _____

3 **Charles Lindbergh   Shakespeare   Louis XIII   Napoleon   Galileo**

He wasn't a pilot, so _____

He wasn't French, so _____

He wasn't a writer, so _____

Answer: _____

4 **the Po   the Amazon   the Danube   the Mississippi   the Rhine**

It's in Europe, so _____

It runs through more than one country, so _____

It doesn't begin with D, so _____

Answer: _____

It hasn't got a trunk so it can't be an elephant . . .

3 Categories

Choose a category of people or things: film stars, characters from soap operas, cars, sports, TV programmes, jobs etc.

The class suggests four names/words which belong to the category and the teacher writes them on the blackboard.

One pupil thinks of one of the names/words.

The other pupils now guess the name/word. They ask questions and make deductions with **can't be** and **must be**.

▶ Sports
  skiing   golf   swimming   sailing

PUPIL A   *Do you do it in water?*
PUPIL B   *No, you don't.*
PUPIL C   *You don't do it in water so it can't be swimming or sailing. Do you do it in the mountains?*
PUPIL B   *No, you don't.*
PUPIL D   *You don't do it in the mountains so it can't be skiing. It must be golf.*

4 The helicopter ride

Complete the sentences with **so** or **such**.

NICK   Uncle Joe is ▶ *Such* a nice uncle. He's ▶ *So* kind. He always has ___1___ good ideas. The helicopter trip was ___2___ a surprise.

JENNY   Yes, it was ___3___ exciting. I didn't realize that London is ___4___ a huge city. There are ___5___ many famous places to see.

NICK   And they all looked ___6___ small from the air. We flew ___7___ close to Big Ben that we could almost touch it. And we flew ___8___ low over Tower Bridge that I thought we were going to land on it.

JENNY   Yes. It was ___9___ fun with Uncle Joe. I enjoyed the trip ___10___ much.

NICK   I got ___11___ a fright when you tried to fly the helicopter. But next time I won't be ___12___ scared.

5 Holiday complaints

Read the complaints about people's holidays and say them in one sentence with **so . . . that**.

▶ It was very cold. We had to wear coats.
  It was so cold that we had to wear coats.

1   The hotel disco was loud. We couldn't sleep.
2   The hotel food was bad. We became ill.
3   Our room was small. We could hardly move.
4   The sea was dirty. We couldn't swim in it.
5   The beach was crowded. We had to walk over people.
6   The shops were expensive. We spent all our money.
7   The hotel waiters were slow. Our food was always cold.
8   It rained a lot. Our clothes were always wet.
9   The pool was small. There wasn't room to swim.
10   The taxis were expensive. We had to walk everywhere.

14 They are both from Liverpool   both, neither; all, none

Power

Power is a new rock group. They're playing in Merton next Saturday. The guitarists Rod and Jake are **both** from Liverpool. They **both** started their careers as actors, but **neither of them** was a big success. **Both of them** say they are happier as musicians. The singer's name is Nina. She's terrific. **All of them** write songs. And they are **all** vegetarians. **None of them** eats meat. They **all** eat health food and they **all** do yoga. They will be giving free concert tickets to **all** the people who buy their new album.

By Jane Marsh

Grammar lesson

both, neither

We use **both** and **neither** to talk about only two people or things.

both takes a plural affirmative verb. It stands after **be** and before full verbs.
▶ *They are **both** from Liverpool.*
   *They **both** started their careers as actors.*
   ***Both of them** say they are happier as musicians.*

neither usually takes a singular affirmative verb. It usually stands at the beginning of a sentence.
▶ ***Neither of them** was a big success.*

all, none

We use **all** and **none** to talk about more than two people or things. **all** takes a plural verb. It stands after **be** or before a full verb.
▶ *They are **all** vegetarians.*
   *They **all** do yoga.*
   ***All of them** write songs.*

none usually takes a singular verb, but a plural verb is also possible. **none** usually stands at the beginning of a sentence.
▶ ***None of them** eats (eat) meat.*

1 Two robbers

a Imagine that you saw the two robbers in the picture. Answer the policeman's questions with **both of them** or **neither of them**.

▶ Were they tall?
  Yes. Both of them were tall.

▶ Did they have beards?
  No. Neither of them had beards.

1 Were they slim?

   _____

2 Were they wearing masks?

   _____

3 Did they have long hair?

   _____

4 Was one of them over fifty?

   _____

5 Were they wearing raincoats?

   _____

6 Were they wearing hats?

   _____

7 Did one of them have an ear-ring?

   _____

8 Were they wearing dark glasses?

   _____

b Look at the answers with **both** in (**a**). Say them again as in the example.
  ▶ *They were both tall.*

2 You and your neighbour

Look at the boy or girl who is sitting next to you. Talk or think about things that are the same, for example, your looks, your age, what you are wearing, what you like or dislike etc.

a Write four sentences with **both**.
  ▶ *Both of us are fourteen.* OR
    We are both fourteen.

1 _____

2 _____

3 _____

4 _____

b Write four sentences with **neither**.
  ▶ *Neither of us likes classical music.*

1 _____

2 _____

3 _____

4 _____

We are both handsome.

3 Profile of 'Power'

Meet Jake, Nina and Rod.

	Jake, 21	Nina, 20	Rod, 22
From	Liverpool	Manchester	Liverpool
Instrument	guitar	keyboard	guitar
Sport	hiking	parachuting	cycling
Hobby	photography	astronomy	sleeping
Likes	travelling, reading	travelling, horses	travelling
Dislikes	fast food, politics	fast food, mice	fast food
Wants to	go on a world tour	star in a musical	write a big hit
Supports	Greenpeace	Friends of the Earth	Worldwide Fund for Nature

a Say what is the same. Use **all of them** or **none of them**.

▶ Who plays an instrument?
All of them play an instrument.

▶ Who comes from London?
None of them comes from London.

1 Who is under twenty?
2 Who does a sport?
3 Who has dark hair?
4 Who has curly hair?
5 Who likes travelling?
6 Who has a hobby?
7 Who wants to make a film?
8 Who comes from the USA?
9 Who dislikes fast food?
10 Who supports an environmental group?

b Now say the sentences from (**a**) with **all** as in the example.

▶ All of them play an instrument.
They all play an instrument.

4 How are they the same?

a What is the same about these people? Write what they are/were and what they do/did. Use **all** or **both**.

▶ Mozart   Beethoven   Chopin.
They were all composers.
They all composed music.

1 Dali   Renoir   Rembrandt

_____

_____

2 Boris Becker   Monica Seles   Andre Agassi

_____

_____

3 Isaac Newton   Alexander Graham Bell

_____

_____

4 Ayrton Senna   Alain Prost

_____

_____

5 Catherine Deneuve   Michele Pfeiffer

_____

_____

6 Mark Twain   Jules Verne

_____

_____

7 Arnold   Robin   Robert
   Schwarzenegger   Williams   De Niro

_____

_____

b Say what is the same about these things. Use **both** or **all**.

▶ Madrid   Seville
They are both Spanish cities.

1 seagull   crow
2 Vienna   Athens   Rome
3 polar bear   arctic hare
4 MTV   BBC   CNN
5 apples   oranges
6 Australia   Sicily   Tahiti
7 Volvo   Ford   Citroën
8 kangaroo   koala

5 Guessing game

A pupil thinks of two other pupils in the class and describes what is the same with **both of them** and **neither of them**.
The class must guess who the two pupils are.

▶ *Both of them are wearing red T-shirts.*
  Neither of them is sitting near the door.

AMANDA I don't think I get enough pocket money. I need more.

NICK Everyone needs more. But **if** lots of people **bought** our newspaper, we **would** soon **be** rich.

JENNY **If** you **had** more money, what **would** you **do** with it?

NICK **If I had** more, **I would spend** more!

AMANDA That's stupid. **If I got** more, **I would save** more.

NICK **If I were** you, **I'd get** a job. **If you went** baby-sitting, you **could earn** money. I could baby-sit, too.

JENNY But you don't like babies.

NICK Well, **I might like** them more **if** they **didn't cry** – and **if** they **played** football.

Grammar lesson

Conditional sentences type 2

We use **if** + past + **would** + infinitive without **to** for situations that are 'unreal'. We imagine a result in the present or future.

▶ *If I **had** more money* (but I haven't),
*I **would** spend more.*
*If you **went** baby-sitting* (but you don't go baby-sitting), *you **would earn** a lot of money.*

When we put the **if** part of the sentence first, we usually use a comma (**,**) after it.

We can also say:

▶ *I **would** spend more **if** I **had** more.*
*You'd **earn** a lot of money **if** you **went** baby-sitting.*

The short form of **would** is **'d**.

Instead of **would** we can use **might** or **could** in the main clause.

▶ *I **might like** them more if they played football.*
(**might** = would possibly)
*If I **got** more, I **could** save more.*
(**could** = would be able to)

After **if** we often use **were** instead of **was** for all persons.

▶ *If I **were** you, I **would get** a job.*

1 What would they do?

Put the verbs in the correct tense and form.

JENNY If Nick got more pocket money,
he ▶ *would waste* _____ (waste) it all on stupid things.

NICK That isn't true. If I had more money,
I [1]_____ (spend) it on a leather jacket.

TOM If I [2]_____ (win) a lottery, I would buy a
CD-player.

NICK I [3]_____ (not buy) a CD-player,
if I were you. They're much too expensive.

JENNY If I had more money, I [4]_____ (save)
it for a trip to Australia.

NICK If I [5]_____ (have) a lot of money,
I [6]_____ (buy) a motor bike.

TOM I [7]_____ (not buy) a motor bike if I
[8]_____ (be) you. They are too dangerous.

NICK If we [9]_____ (not get) so much homework,
I [10]_____ (deliver) newspapers every
morning.

TOM What has homework got to do with a morning
paper-round?

JENNY Well, you see, Nick does his homework between getting up
and eating breakfast.

---

2 If …

a   What **would** or **wouldn't** you do, if you got more
pocket money? Write five sentences.

▶ *If I got more pocket money, I would buy more clothes.*
▶ *If I got more pocket money, I wouldn't complain so much.*

1 _____

2 _____

3 _____

4 _____

5 _____

b   If you could spend a day with a famous person,
who would you choose? What would you do?
Where would you go? What would you talk
about?

Say four sentences.

▶ *If I could spend a day with a famous person, I
would choose Julia Roberts. I would go to
Hollywood with her …*

3 Just imagine . . .

a What do you think you **would** do if these things happened? Write your answers.

▶ if you found a big hairy spider in your bed
  (a) scream
  b squash it
  c keep it as a pet

  If I found a big hairy spider in my bed, I would scream.

1 if you saw a famous actor in the street
  a go up and say hello
  b be too shy to speak
  c follow him or her

2 if you saw a strange object in the sky
  a photograph it
  b tell your friends
  c call the police

3 if you found a bag full of money under a tree
  a spend it
  b tell the police
  c share it with your friends

4 if you heard a loud noise in the night
  a hide under the bed
  b get up and look
  c go to sleep again

5 if you saw an elephant walking down the street
  a phone the zoo
  b run the other way
  c do nothing

6 if you were alone on a desert island
  a cry
  b explore it
  c look out for a ship

7 if you found a snake in your cupboard
  a run away
  b pick it up
  c shut the door

8 if you suddenly saw yourself on television
  a laugh
  b record it
  c turn the television off

9 if the phone rang in the middle of the night
  a get out of bed and answer it
  b put the pillow over your head
  c tell someone to answer it

10 if you won a car
  a sell it
  b give it to someone in your family
  c keep it until you got your driving licence

b Do the exercise again. This time, say what you **wouldn't do**.

▶ *If I found a big spider in my bed, I wouldn't keep as a pet.*

4 If it happened to me . . .

The following things might happen. What **would** you do if they happened to you? Write your answers.

▶ If I found a gold ring in the street,
I would give it to my sister.

1   If my best friend moved to another town,

2   If I lost my voice,

3   If I saw someone hurt in an accident,

4   If someone offered me a Saturday job in a butcher's shop,

5   If all the lights suddenly went out,

6   If the television broke down in the middle of my favourite programme,

7   If I found a purse full of money in a bus,

8   If I spilled orange juice on my English homework,

5 The tropical island game

Choose two things from the list that you would do if you lived on a tropical island for six months. Write two sentences.

sleep all day	build a boat
climb palm trees	go fishing all day
play with the monkeys	live in a tree house
collect shells	swim every day
learn the local language	explore the jungle
write a book about it	paint pictures of it

▶ *If I lived on a tropical island, I would climb palm trees.*

1

2

The other pupils must take turns to guess what you have chosen. They can only have a second guess if they get the first one right.

▶ PUPIL   *If you lived on a tropical island you would climb palm trees.*

　YOU   *Yes, I would.* (He or she can ask another question.) OR *No, I wouldn't.*

The first pupil to guess both answers correctly then takes your place.

Grammar lesson

Relative clauses

who, **which**, **that** and **whose** are relative pronouns. They introduce relative clauses.

▶   *Roberto is the boy **who** lived next door.*

We use **who** for people and **which** for things. We can also use **that** for people and things.

When **who/which/that** is the object of the relative clause, we can leave it out.

▶   *This is the **photo I like best**.*
    (OR *the photo **which/that** I like best*)
    *I always take photos of **people I meet**.*
    (OR *people **who/that** I meet*)

To show possession we use **whose**.

▶   *Is that the boy **whose** sister is a scientist?*

Prepositions (**in, from** etc.) come at the end of the relative clause.

▶   *I always take photos of **places we stay at**.*

JENNY   Here are our holiday photos from Italy. That's the village **which** we stayed **in.** And that's Roberto, the boy **who** lived next door.

JANE   Oh, is that the boy **whose** sister is a scientist? You told me about him.

JENNY   Yes, that's right. He was great fun. We had a good time.

JANE   I always take photos of **people I meet** on holiday and **places we stay at.**

JENNY   But this is **the photo I like best.** It's one of **the funniest I've ever taken.** We were eating in a restaurant when Nick's chair broke. He fell and his face went right into his plate of spaghetti.

1 Food facts

Some of these facts about food are wrong.
Complete the sentences with **which** or **who**.
Then write **T** in the box if you think it is true or
F if you think it is false.

| T | The food ► *which* we eat gives us energy.

| ☐ | There are thousands of chemical changes
¹_____ happen in our bodies every
second.

| ☐ | People ²_____ do sports need less
energy.

| ☐ | Carrots are vegetables ³_____ make
your hair curly.

| ☐ | Meat, cheese, eggs, fish and milk are foods
⁴_____ give us protein.

| ☐ | People ⁵_____ want to lose weight
should eat lots of sugar, cream and butter.

| ☐ | In the past, people ate the food ⁶_____
grew where they lived.

| ☐ | Today we eat food ⁷_____ comes from
all over the world.

| ☐ | Vitamins are things ⁸_____ we need in
very large amounts.

| ☐ | People ⁹_____ sleep all day use a lot of
energy.

| ☐ | Oranges are fruit ¹⁰_____ contain a lot
of vitamin C.

| ☐ | Food ¹¹_____ is fresh contains more
vitamins.

| ☐ | A person ¹²_____ eats an apple a day will
never be ill.

2 Charles Dickens

What do you know about Charles Dickens?
Complete the sentences with **who**, **which** or
whose. If **who** and **which** are not necessary,
don't write them in.

Charles Dickens was an English writer
► *who* lived from 1812 to 1870. The books
► ⁄ he wrote are read in many countries.

Dickens, ¹_____ family was very poor, had to
start work when he was ten years old. In
England at that time, people ²_____ could
not pay their debts were sent to prison. This
happened to Dickens' father, ³_____ first
name was John. This meant that Dickens,
⁴_____ was only a boy, had to visit his father
in prison.

Later, Dickens wrote books based on people
⁵_____ he had known and places ⁶_____
he had lived in. In 'David Copperfield' he
wrote about the visits ⁷_____ he paid to his
father in prison. In some of his books he wrote
about terrible schools like the one ⁸_____ he
went to himself . In 'Oliver Twist' he wrote
about children ⁹_____ were poor and
sometimes orphans – children ¹⁰_____
parents have died.

Dickens is known for making up characters like
Uriah Heep, Fagin and the Artful Dodger,
¹¹_____ names are known even to some
people ¹²_____ have not read the books.

Dickens, ¹³_____ was also a good actor, used
to read his stories to audiences in England and
America.

He married a woman ¹⁴_____ name was
Catherine and ¹⁵_____ was the daughter of
his first publisher.

3 USA quiz

Amanda has written a quiz for the newspaper.
Can you do it? Put in **who**, **which** or **whose**.
Then ring the correct answer.

▶ What is the name of the big river _which_

flows through the United States?

   a   the Volga
   (b) the Mississippi
   c   the Seine

1 What is the name of the bridge _____ is

built over the San Francisco Bay?

   a   Brooklyn Bridge
   b   the Golden Gate Bridge
   c   Tower Bridge

2 What is the name of the baseball team

_____ home city is New York?

   a   the New York Yankees
   b   the Cincinatti Reds
   c   the Chicago Bears

3 Who was the famous American _____

invented the lightbulb?

   a   Thomas Edison
   b   Henry Ford
   c   Bill Cosby

4 What is the name of the waterfall _____

is between the US and Canada?

   a   the Angel Falls
   b   the Victoria Falls
   c   the Niagara Falls

5 Who was the president _____ ended

slavery?

   a   George Washington
   b   Ulysees S. Grant
   c   Abraham Lincoln

6 What is the name of the city in the desert

_____ is famous for its casinos and shows?

   a   Los Angeles
   b   Las Vegas
   c   Santa Fe

7 What is the name of the famous singer

_____ big house near Memphis is called
Graceland?

   a   Elvis Presley
   b   Louis Armstrong
   c   Jimi Hendrix

8 Name one of the presidents _____

heads are carved in Mount Rushmore.

   a   Washington
   b   Nixon
   c   Carter

9 What is the name of the man _____

became a famous outlaw in the 'Wild West'?

   a   Jesse James
   b   Columbo
   c   Fred Astaire

10 What is the name of the state _____

once belonged to Russia?

   a   Hawaii
   b   Washington
   c   Alaska

4 I know someone whose . . .

Make up some funny facts about someone (true
or untrue). Play this game round the class. Use
whose . . .

▶ PUPIL A *I know someone whose brother has seen
a spaceship.*

  PUPIL B *I know someone whose brother has seen
a spaceship and whose grandmother
writes pop music.*

  PUPIL C *I know someone whose brother has seen
a spaceship, whose grandmother writes
pop music and whose grandfather
rides a motor bike.*

  PUPIL D *I know someone whose . . .*

5 What's the same?

Match up the pairs and say what is the same.
Make sentences with a preposition at the end.

▶ *A knife and a spoon are things we eat with.*

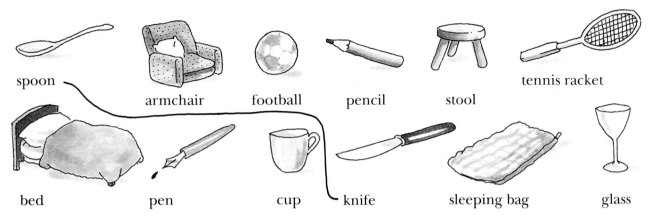

spoon   armchair   football   pencil   stool   tennis racket

bed   pen   cup   knife   sleeping bag   glass

---

6 Things and people

a   Read the clues and fill in the crossword puzzle.

Across

▶ You keep money in it.
5 You stick paper with it.
7 You buy newspapers and magazines from him/her.
9 You buy medicine from him/her.
10 You put flowers in it.
11 You eat with it.
13 You sleep outdoors in it.
14 You go to him/her when you're ill.
15 You sew with it.

Down

1 You drive in it.
2 You pack clothes in it.
3 You go to him/her when your tooth hurts.
4 You learn English from him/her.
6 You laugh at it.
8 You wash your hair with it.
12 You bake food in it.
13 You repair things with it.

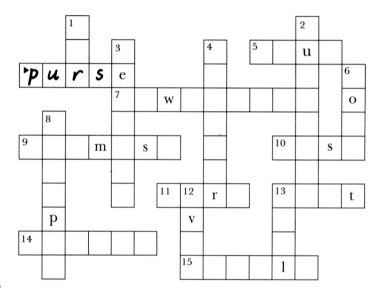

b   Ask questions round the class about the things
and people in the puzzle. Do not use a relative
pronoun. Don't forget the preposition.

▶ YOU   *What's the thing you keep money in?*
   PUPIL *A purse.*
▶ YOU   *Who's the person you go to when you're ill?*
   PUPIL *A doctor.*

need/want + ing; have/get something done

AMANDA   My hair looks terrible. Do you think it **needs cutting**? Or does it just **want washing**? The last time I **had it cut** I looked like a boy.

JENNY   Don't **have it cut**. **Get it permed**. Then you'll look like the model in this magazine.

Grammar lesson

need/want + ing

After **need** and **want** we use an **ing** form to suggest that something should be done to a person or thing.

▶ *My hair needs cutting.*
   (I/Someone should cut my hair.)
   My hair wants washing.
   (I/Someone should wash my hair.)

have/get something done

We use **have** + object + past participle to say that somebody does a job for us. We do not do it ourselves.

▶ *Shall I have my hair cut?*
   Don't have it done. Do it yourself.

Be careful with the word order. Compare:

▶ *I had my hair cut.*
   (= past simple, the hairdresser cut it.)
   I had cut my hair.
   (= past perfect, I cut my hair myself.)

Sometimes **get** is used instead of **have**.

▶ *Get it permed.*

1 What needs doing?

a   Complete the sentences with **need** and a word from the box.

clean	iron	shorten
comb	pump up	wash ✓
mow	repair	polish
feed	mend	

▶   Nick's socks   *need washing*.
1   Ben's finger-nails _____
2   Tom's jeans _____
3   Amanda's boots _____
4   Nick's hair _____
5   The tyre _____
6   Mike's shirt _____
7   Jenny's dress _____
8   The washing machine _____
9   Chip _____
10   The grass _____

b   Do the exercise again with **want** and the words from the box.

▶ *His socks want washing.*

2 What are they having done?

a Look at the picture of the fair and use the words from
the box with **have** to make sentences.

tattoo	tell
read	take
draw	paint
guess ✓	

▶ Mrs Bell *is having her weight guessed.*

1 Jane _____

2 Tom _____

3 Ben _____

4 Amanda and Jenny _____

5 Nick _____

6 Trig _____

b With a partner, ask and answer five questions about what you
have had done. Use the ideas from (**a**) or some of your own.

▶ YOU 　　*Have you ever had your fortune told?*
　 PARTNER *No, I haven't, but I would like to have my fortune told.* OR
　　　　　　Yes, I have.

3 Mr and Mrs Rich

Mr Rich is a millionaire and a very busy man.
He and his wife don't do much themselves.
They have everything done for them.
Read the questions and write Mr Rich's answers.

▶ Do you make your appointments yourself?
(my secretary)

No, I don't. I have my appointments made by my secretary.

▶ Does your wife do her hair herself?
(her hairdresser)

No, she doesn't. She has her hair done by her hairdresser.

1 Do you answer your letters yourself?
(my secretary)

_____

2 Does your wife do the shopping herself?
(our housekeeper)

_____

3 Do you arrange interviews yourself?
(my assistant)

_____

4 Does your wife do the housework herself?
(our maid)

_____

5 Do you write your speeches yourself?
(my assistant)

_____

6 Do you plan your business trips yourself?
(my secretary)

_____

7 Do you fly your helicopter yourself?
(our pilot)

_____

8 Does your wife make her clothes herself?
(designers)

_____

9 Do you do the gardening yourselves?
(our gardener)

_____

10 Do you do the cooking yourselves?
(our cook)

_____

4 Why don't you . . . ?

Complete the dialogues by making suggestions
with **Why don't you** and the words from the box.

Why don't you have
your hair permed?

service	test (× 2) ✓
cut	mend
examine	alter
type	paint
fill	dye

▶ BEN   I can't see a thing.

   NICK   *Why don't you have your eyes tested?*

1   TOM   My hair's too long.

   JENNY   _____

2   MIKE   My car isn't running very well.

   TOM   _____

3   NICK   I have got toothache.

   BEN   _____

4   JANE   This skirt is too loose. It looks terrible.

   JENNY   _____

5   JENNY   Our dog has been acting strangely.
          I don't think he's well.

   AMANDA   _____

6   JANE   I hate the colour of this dress.

   JENNY   _____

7   NICK   What did you say? I can't hear a thing.

   JENNY   _____

8   AMANDA   I've just written a very long essay but
          nobody can read my handwriting.

   JENNY   _____

9   TOM   I've got a big tear in my jacket.

   MIKE   _____

10   NICK   Dave's car looks very rusty.

   TOM   _____

18 Nick told Ben ...   Indirect questions; Indirect commands and requests

Newspaper meeting, Thursday at lunch time.

> Is the USA quiz finished?

> Nick, there's a . . .

> Don't interrupt.

Jenny **asked if** the USA quiz **was** finished. Nick **told** Ben **not to interrupt**.

> When will the questionnaire on smoking be finished?

> Nick, can't you see . . .

> Ben, wait your turn please!

Tom **asked when** the questionnaire on smoking **would** be finished. Nick **asked** Ben to wait his turn.

> Have you done your interview Tom?

> But Nick, your . . .

> Shut up Ben!

Jenny **wanted to know whether** Tom **had done** his interview. Nick **told** Ben **to shut up**.

> What did you want to tell Nick?

> I just wanted to tell him that there was a worm in his salad. It's too late now.

Grammar lesson

Indirect questions

1 In indirect questions the word order is not the same as in direct questions. It is the same as in statements.
   We do not use **do/does/did** to make indirect questions. We do not put a question mark at the end.

2 If there is no question word (**who, when** etc.) in the direct question, we begin the indirect question with **if** or **whether**.
   ▶ *'Is the USA quiz finished?'* (direct question)
   Jenny asked if the quiz was finished. (indirect question)

3 Reporting verbs for indirect questions are **ask**, **want to know**, **wonder**. The change of tenses is the same as for indirect statements.

present	→	past
past	→	past perfect
present perfect	→	past perfect
past perfect	→	no change
will	→	**would**
may	→	**might**
shall	→	**should**
can	→	**could**

4 If there is a question word in the direct question, we repeat it in the indirect question.
   ▶ *'**When will** the questionnaire on smoking be finished?'* (direct)
   *He asked **when** the questionnaire **would** be finished.* (indirect)

Indirect commands and requests

1 We form indirect commands with **tell** + person + **to** + infinitive.
   ▶ *Nick said, 'Shut up, Ben.'*
      *Nick **told** Ben **to** shut up.*

   We use **not to** for negative commands.
   ▶ *Nick said, 'Don't interrupt.'*
      *Nick **told** Ben **not to interrupt**.*

2 We can make indirect requests with **ask** + person + **to** + infinitive.
   ▶ *Nick said, 'Ben, wait your turn, please.'*
      *Nick **asked** Ben **to wait** his turn.*

Are you all right?

Yesterday, Jane saw a little boy who had fallen off his bicycle. She went to help him and asked him some questions.

What did she ask him? Ring the question word first, if there is one, then report Jane's question. Remember the word order and the changes of tense and pronouns.

▶ '(What's) your name?'
   She asked him what his name was.

▶ 'Are you all right?'
   She asked him if he was all right.

1 'How old are you?'

   _____

2 'Where do you live?'

   _____

3 'Have you hurt yourself?'

   _____

4 'Can you stand up?'

   _____

5 'Is your elbow bleeding?'

   _____

6 'How did it happen?'

   _____

7 'What made you fall?'

   _____

8 'Where had you been?'

   _____

9 'Were you on the way home?'

   _____

10 'Shall I phone your parents?'

   _____

11 'Do you want some help?'

   _____

12 'Shall I take you home?'

   _____

2 What do you do?

a Nick is interviewing Jumping Jake Jones, a professional wrestler on tour in Merton. Read his questions and write them in indirect form.

▶ 'How much do you weigh?'

He asked him how much
he weighed.

▶ 'How many times have you been on television?'

He asked him how many times
he had been on television.

1 'How did you start wrestling?'

_____

_____

2 'How long have you been a professional wrestler?'

_____

_____

3 'Who is your favourite opponent?'

_____

_____

4 'How many wins have you had?'

_____

_____

5 'How many kilos can you lift?'

_____

_____

6 'Is it difficult to become a professional wrestler?'

_____

_____

7 'What do you think about violent sports?'

_____

_____

8 'Is Jumping Jake Jones your real name?'

_____

_____

9 'How many times have you fought this year?'

_____

_____

10 'Will you stay in Merton all week?'

_____

_____

11 'Who is the best wrestler in the world?'

_____

_____

12 'Which was your best fight?'

_____

_____

13 'Have you been to Merton before?'

_____

_____

14 'How can I become the strongest boy at school?'

_____

_____

b Your partner writes five interview questions for one of the people below. You tell the class what your partner wanted to know.

▶ Mr Flip, how long have you been training dolphins?

YOU *He wanted to know how long Mr Flip had been training dolphins.*

Miss Starr
Astrologer

Mr Flip
Dolphin trainer

Trevor Top
Wig designer

Ms Mavis Mumm
Mime artist

Fire!

Can you remember what these instructions tell you to do? Read instruction one then close your book and tell your partner. Do the same for instructions two and three.

▶ *It tells you to turn off electrical equipment before you go out.*
It tells you not to put papers close to heaters . . .

1 How to prevent a fire

- Turn off electrical equipment before you go out.
- Do not put papers close to heaters.
- Be careful near an open fire.
- Buy a smoke detector.
- Do not put lit cigarettes in the bin.

2 What to do in case of a small fire

- Put it out if possible.
- Get everyone out of the building.
- Call the fire brigade.
- Do not open the windows.
- Shut doors.

3 What to do if caught in a fire

- Don't panic.
- Shout so people know where you are.
- Don't jump out of the window if it is too high.
- Put a damp cloth over your mouth.
- Wave so that people can see you.

He asked Jane to feed his fish

Mike was getting ready to go away. He asked people to help him. Who did he ask to do what? Say the answers.

▶ 'Will you get my suitcase from the spare room?'
He asked Ben to get his suitcase from the spare room.

▶ 'Please don't forget to feed my goldfish.'
He asked Jane not to forget to feed his goldfish.

1 'Can you lend me your backpack?'
2 'Will you fetch me a Chinese take-away?'
3 'Don't use my CD-player, please!'
4 'Can you make me some coffee?'
5 'Will you buy me some toothpaste?'
6 'Will you water my plants?'
7 'Will you iron this shirt for me?'
8 'Can you phone the airport?'

19 You ought to turn it down

ought to, **should**; Phrasal verbs

JENNY Nick, Mum has a headache. We **ought to be** quiet. We **shouldn't make** so much noise.

NICK Did you say something?

JENNY The music is too loud. You **ought to turn it down**.

NICK I can't hear you!

JENNY Don't shout, Nick! **Shut up**! And **turn the music down**!

NICK Yes, I've already been to town.

JENNY No, Nick. Your music. **Turn down your music**!

NICK I can't hear you. The music's too loud.

1 You ought to do it

Some of your friends have problems. Give advice with **ought to**.

Use these or your own ideas:

go to bed earlier	talk to them
join a club	work harder
see a doctor	wear glasses
get a job	save money for a new
go on a diet	one
tidy it	get it cut

▶ I'm always tired.
   You ought to go to bed earlier.
1 My eyes are sometimes red and sore.
2 I never have enough money.
3 My school marks are bad.
4 I'm too fat.
5 I've got spots.
6 I've had a quarrel with my parents.
7 I haven't got many friends.
8 My old bicycle needs repairing again.
9 My hair looks terrible.
10 I can't find anything. My room is so untidy.

Grammar lesson

ought to, should

We use **ought to** + infinitive or **should** + infinitive to give advice or to say what we think is right. **ought to** means the same as **should**. In question and negative forms, we use **should** more than **ought to**.

I **should** go	I **shouldn't** go	**Should** I g̲o̲
I **ought** to go ———		———

Phrasal verbs

1 Phrasal verbs are formed with a verb + adverb (for example, **down**, **up**, **on**, **off**)

verb + adverb
turn   **down**

2 Sometimes the meaning is clear (for example, **stand up**, **sit down**, **turn** something **down**, **turn** something **on**). Often, the two words together have a special meaning which we cannot guess.
   ▶ *Shut up!* (= be quiet, stop talking)

3 Sometimes a phrasal verb has an object. If the object is a noun, it can stand befor̲e̲ or after the adverb:
   ▶ *Turn **the music** down.*
      *Turn down **the music**.*

But if the object is a pronoun (**him**, **her**, **it**, **them**) it must stand between the verb and the adverb:
   ▶ *Turn **it** down!*

4 Look at these phrasal verbs.

put something **on**
   ▶ *Nick is **putting on** his jacket.*
      *He is **putting it on**.*

take something **off**
   ▶ *Tom is **taking off** his football boots.*
      *He is **taking them off**.*

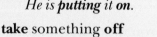

Should stars earn so much money?

No. All pop stars and sports stars ought to give money to charities. What they do is only for themselves. People such as nurses and teachers ought to earn more because they help others.

LIZ

Stars shouldn't earn so much. Some of them haven't even had a proper education. Scientists and people who have studied at universities ought to earn more.

KEN

Why not? Film stars and sports stars work hard at their jobs and they entertain millions of people. They deserve their money. Of course they ought to live in luxury.

DAVID

Stars should earn a lot because they make you believe anything is possible. They can make you dream. Dentists and lawyers ought to be paid less.

MARY

a **What do they think?**
Say answers with **ought to** or **shouldn't**.

▶ What does Liz think about nurses and teachers?
She thinks that nurses and teachers ought to earn more.

1 What does Mary think about being a star?
2 What does Ken think about stars?
3 What does David think about film stars and sports stars?
4 What does Ken think about people who have studied?
5 What does Liz think about pop stars and sports stars?
6 What does Mary think about dentists and lawyers?

b Who do you agree with?

▶ *I agree with Ken that people who have studied ought to earn more.*

_____

_____

c Think about the work that these people do.

pilots	kindergarten teachers
toy makers	social workers
fashion designers	nurses
astronauts	scientists
engineers	

Who ought to earn more? Why?
Who ought to earn less? Why?
Write your answers.

_____

_____

_____

_____

_____

_____

3 Job advice

Your partner must say what he/she would like
to be one day. You say what he/she **ought to** do.

▶ PARTNER   *I would like to be a doctor.*
   YOU   *You ought to study medicine.*
▶ PARTNER   *I would like to be a window-cleaner.*
   YOU   *You ought to buy a bucket.*

---

4 What do you do?

Put the correct phrasal verb in the box. Then
say what you do with the things.

fill in ✓	try on
turn on/off	throw away
take off	write down

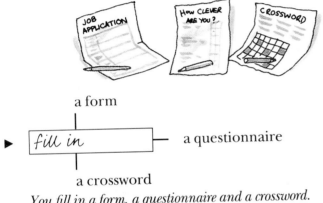

a form

▶ | fill in | ─ a questionnaire

a crossword

You fill in a form, a questionnaire and a crossword.

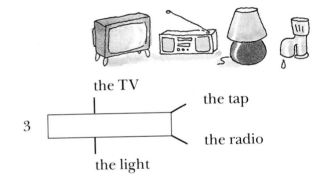

the TV

the tap

3 | |

the radio

the light

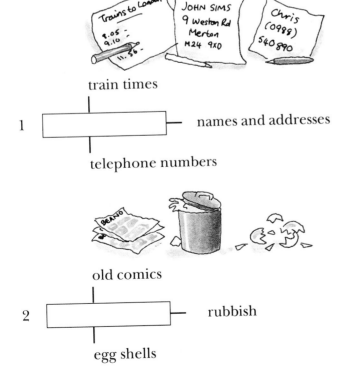

train times

1 | | ─ names and addresses

telephone numbers

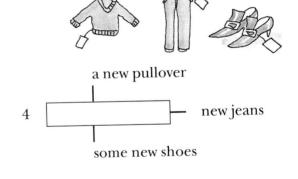

a new pullover

4 | | ─ new jeans

some new shoes

old comics

2 | | ─ rubbish

egg shells

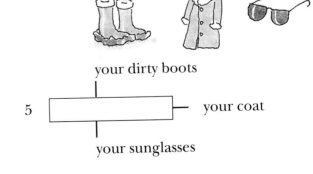

your dirty boots

5 | | ─ your coat

your sunglasses

5 Fill it in

Complete the sentences and fill in the crossword.

Across

► Don't stand up. Sit *down* !

3 You've left the oven on. Turn it _____ , please.

5 The light's too bright. _____ it off.

6 It's very cold outside. _____ your jacket on.

8 When must I take these library books _____ ?

Down

1 Come _____ ! We're late!

2 That coat looks awful. Take it _____ .

3 It's too dark in here. Turn the light _____ , please.

4 I'm going to throw these broken toys _____ .

5 Your shoes are muddy. _____ them off.

7 What time do you get _____ every morning?

---

6 I've already taken them off

Answer the requests with **already** and replace the underlined words with **it** or **them**. Make sure that you get the word order right.

► Take your dirty shoes off. I've just washed the floor.
   I've already taken them off.

► Turn up the volume, please.
   I've already turned it up.

1 Take your books back to the library.

   _____

2 Look her number up in the phone book.

   _____

3 Write down the words in your notebook.

   _____

4 Try on the shoes before you pay for them.

   _____

5 Turn the lights off in your room.

   _____

6 Turn down the heat. It's much too hot.

   _____

7 Clean up the mess you left in the kitchen.

   _____

8 Don't forget to fill in those forms.

   _____

9 Put on your best clothes. We're going out.

   _____

10 Bring the dirty glasses down from your room.

   _____

20 I wish my nose was shorter

Question tags; **wish** + past simple; Plural nouns

JENNY   I wish my nose **was** shorter. **It's** too long, **isn't it**?

AMANDA   I wish I **didn't have** so many freckles. **They're** silly-looking, **aren't they**?

JENNY   I like them. I wish I **was** taller. **I'm not** tall enough, **am I**?

AMANDA   I wish I **didn't wear** glasses. They look stupid, **don't they**? They **don't** really suit me, **do they**?

JENNY   Yes they do. I wish I **had** glasses. I like your new jeans, too. You bought them yesterday, **didn't you**?

AMANDA   Yes, from the new shop in South Street.

JENNY   They **didn't** cost much, **did they**?

AMANDA   No, how did you know?

JENNY   Because the price tag is still on them.

Grammar lesson

Question tags

1   We often use a question tag at the end of a sentence when we ask for agreement.

   Sometimes it is not a real question. Then the voice goes down.

▶ *My nose is too long, isn't it?*

   If we ask a real question (because we are not sure), the voice goes up.

▶ *You bought them yesterday, didn't you?*

2   If the statement is affirmative, the question tag is negative.

▶ *Freckles are silly-looking, aren't they?*

   If the statement is negative, the question tag is affirmative:

▶ *I'm not tall enough, am I?*

   But the question tags always end with **I**, **you**, **he**, **she**, **it**, **we** or **they**.

3   If the statement verb is **be**, **have**, **do**, **can**, **must**, **should** etc., we repeat it in the question tag.

   With other verbs we use a form of **do** in the question tag:

▶ *My glasses **look** stupid, **don't they**? They **didn't cost** much, **did they**?*

wish + past simple

We use **wish** + past simple to talk about something in the present that we regret.

▶ *I wish my nose **was** shorter.* (My nose is long.) *I wish I **didn't wear** glasses.* (I wear glasses.) *I wish I **had** glasses.* (But I haven't got glasses.)

Note also: *I wish I could* (do something) . . .

Plural nouns

Some nouns are always plural, so the verb is also plural:

jeans	pyjamas	glasses
trousers	shorts	tights
scissors		

▶ *Your jeans **are** new. I like **them**. Your glasses **look** great. **They** suit you.*

We can also say **a pair of** with **jeans**, **trousers** etc. Then the verb is singular. Compare:

▶ *There **are some** nice **trousers** in the shop window. There **is a** nice **pair of trousers** in the shop window.*

1 It's in France, isn't it?

Ben is writing a quiz about different countries. He isn't sure about the answers and is asking the others. Put in the correct tags.

▶ The 'Louvre' is in Paris, _isn't it_ ?

1 There are about 170 countries in the world, _____ ?

2 Brazil and Italy have both won the World Cup three times, _____ ?

3 About 500 million people live in Europe, _____ ?

4 Alaska is the largest state in the USA, _____ ?

5 There are over 1,300 languages spoken in Africa, _____ ?

6 The population of China makes up one-fifth of the world's population, _____ ?

7 The last emperor of China was called Pu Yi, _____ ?

8 America became independent in 1776, _____ ?

9 There are more people in Mexico City than in any other city in the world, _____ ?

10 In 1923 half of Tokyo was destroyed by an earthquake, _____ ?

2 The basketball match

The school team has just lost a match. Tom is discussing it with Simon. Write the question tags.

SIMON The others were quite good, ▶ _weren't they_ ?

TOM But we played badly, ▶ _didn't we_ ? I didn't play very well, 1_____ ?

SIMON Perhaps not, but Mark scored for the first time, 2_____ ?

TOM Yes, that was a surprise, 3_____ ?

SIMON Actually, we have got some very good players, 4_____ ? There's Tony, and Jim, and Brian . . .

TOM Yes, but they didn't score today, 5_____ ? We couldn't get past their defence, 6_____ ? I was useless too, 7_____ ?

SIMON Well, you missed some training, 8_____ ?

TOM Yes, I did . . . If we lose the next match, we won't go to the finals, 9_____ ?

SIMON Oh yes, we will. Because you aren't going to miss any more training sessions, 10_____ ?

3 Regrets

What are they thinking?
Make sentences with **I wish** + past simple.

▶ Nick is at the back of the queue.
I wish I was at the front of the queue OR
I wish I wasn't at the back of the queue.

1 Jane is ill.

_____

2 Sue has straight hair.

_____

3 Nick can't dance.

_____

4 Ben doesn't know how to repair his Walkman.

_____

5 The boots are too expensive for Amanda.

_____

6 Jane can't afford the ear-rings.

_____

4 I wish I was taller

a Do you ever wish that some things were different? Write two sentences with **I wish I had**, two with **I wish I was** and two with **I wish I could**.

▶ *I wish I had red shoes.*
▶ *I wish I was taller.*
▶ *I wish I could sing in tune.*

1 _____
2 _____
3 _____
4 _____
5 _____
6 _____

b Choose one thing from each list which you wish you were, had, or could do. Write them on a piece of paper.

> *I wish I was famous.*
> *I wish I had a credit card.*
> *I wish I could tell the future.*

In pairs, ask and answer questions with **Do you wish you were/had/could** until you find out what your partner has written.

were
a millionaire
famous
older
in the Guinness Book of Records

had
a driving licence
some diving equipment
a credit card
a photographic memory

could
become invisible
tell the future
appear on a TV game show
invent clever machines

▶ YOU   *Do you wish you were a millionaire?*
   PARTNER   *No, I don't.*

5 Are those new?

Jane and Amanda are shopping. Decide if the words in boxes should be singular or plural and cross out the wrong word.

JANE   ▶ | Is/Are | those new sunglasses?

AMANDA   Yes. | 1 They/It | | 2 is/are | nice, | 3 aren't/isn't |

| 4 it/they | ? Nick gave | 5 it/them | to me. It's a shame I can't

see very well out of | 6 it/them | . Everything looks funny.

JANE   Look at | 7 that/those | red trousers.

AMANDA   The | 8 one/ones | beside the T-shirts?

JANE   No. | 9 Those/That | | 10 is/are | a pair of yellow pyjamas.

AMANDA   Oh. What a lovely blue skirt that is.

JANE | 11 That/Those | | 12 is/are | a pair of pink shorts.

AMANDA | 13 They/It | would go well with | 14 those/that | striped

tights. And look at | 15 that/those | jeans! I would love

| 16 a/some | pair of them.

JANE | 17 This/Those | | 18 is/are | the yellow pyjamas again!

Amanda, did Nick tell you what kind of sunglasses | 19 they/it |

| 20 is/are | ?

21 Has the thief been found? The passive: simple forms

TOM The newsagent's **has been broken into**. About £850 **has been taken**.

NICK **Has** the thief **been found**?

TOM No, not yet. The theft **was** only **discovered** an hour ago. There's a room at the back of the shop where the money **is kept** in a safe. This morning the cleaner noticed that the window **had been broken**, so she told the owner. A few people **have been questioned** by the police, but nobody knows much. An officer said that any information **will be welcomed**.

NICK Will there be a reward?

Grammar lesson

The passive: simple forms

1 Form: **be** + past participle

present	money	**is**	kept
past	the theft	**was**	discovered
present perfect	£850	**has been**	taken
past perfect	a window	**had been**	broken
future	information	**will be**	welcomed

Object

Active Somebody **stole** £850 from the newsagent's.

Passive £850 **was stolen** from the newsagent's.

Subject

2 We use the passive if we do not know who does something, or if it is not important or not necessary to say who does it.

3 We can use **by** + person/thing if we wish to say who or what did the action.
  ▶ *A few people have been questioned **by the police**.*

1 Were you asked?

Can you match the form of the passive in each sentence with the name of the passive tense?

Have you been invited?

▶ Were you asked? — **present passive**

▶ I am invited. — **past passive**

1 Is Greek spoken?

2 The room hadn't been cleaned.

3 She won't be asked.

4 Has the window been broken?

5 She wasn't injured.

6 I haven't been informed.

7 He will be punished.

8 Has the money been found?

9 When was the house built?

10 Will I be invited?

11 English is spoken here.

12 He was killed in an accident.

13 These toys are made in China.

14 Had the parcel been opened?

present perfect passive

past perfect passive

future passive

---

2 At the doctor's

Write what happens when you go to the doctor's. Use the present simple passive.

▶ He tests your eyes.
  Your eyes are tested.

1 He looks at your throat.

2 He takes your pulse.

3 He weighs you.

4 He checks your blood pressure.

5 He examines your chest.

6 He X-rays your lungs.

7 He takes a blood sample.

8 He measures your height.

9 He tests your hearing.

10 He listens to your heart.

3 What has been done?

An old street in Merton has been modernized.
Use the words from the box to write what has been done in
the present perfect passive.

Last year

Now

build	
widen	
paint	
plant	
provide (×2)	
pull down	
put up	
repair	
take away	
turn into ✓	

▶ The street *has been turned into a pedestrian zone.*

1 Street lamps _____

2 Trees and flowers _____

3 The pavement _____

4 A fountain _____

5 Litter bins _____

6 The bus stop _____

7 The old house _____

8 The shops _____

9 The holes in the road _____

10 Benches _____

4 Krakatoa

Put the verbs in brackets into the past simple passive.

Did you know that the greatest explosion in the world

▶ _was caused_ (cause) by a volcano? Krakatoa, an island in

Indonesia, erupted in 1883. More than half the island

1 _____ (destroy). The explosion 2 _____

(hear) in India and Australia. Rocks 3 _____ (throw)

more than 55 kilometres high into the air. Surprisingly, only a few

people 4 _____ (kill), but a huge wave, 35 metres high,

5 _____ (create) by the explosion. Several small islands

6 _____ (cover) by the wave. 163 villages

7 _____ (destroy) and 36,000 people

8 _____ (drown). Dust 9 _____ (carry) all

round the world, and the weather everywhere 10 _____

(affect) for many years afterwards.

---

5 What had been changed?

When the pupils went back to school after the summer
holidays, a lot of things had been changed.
Write the words in brackets in the past perfect passive.

▶ New desks _had been bought_ (buy).

1   A lot of trees _____ (plant).

2   New lights _____ (put in).

3   The classrooms _____ (paint).

4   A tennis court _____ (build).

5   The fence _____ (taken down).

6   Five new classrooms _____ (add).

7   New equipment _____ (buy) for the chemistry lab.

8   Showers _____ (install) in the changing rooms.

9   New blackboards _____ (put up) in the classrooms.

10 The whole school _____ (modernize).

6 Graffiti competition

Put the verbs into the future passive.

Graffiti competition

A graffiti competition ▸ _will be held_ (hold) next week for all Merton's young artists. The age limit is fifteen.

All competitors [1]_____ (invite) to attend a graffiti session in the town hall from 2 pm to 6 pm on Saturday the ninth of September. Competitors [2]_____ (ask) to create graffiti designs for the entrance of the new town hall, which [3]_____ (open) at the beginning of the month.

Large sheets of paper and spray paint [4]_____ (provide).

Entries [5]_____ (judge) by five professional artists.

Winners [6]_____ (contacted) by telephone on the thirteenth of September. The names of the winners [7]_____ (print) in 'Merton News' on the fifteenth of September.

Three prizes of £50, £30, £20 [8]_____ (award).
Prizes [9]_____ (present) by the Mayor.
The winner [10]_____ (invite) to spray paint the entrance hall of the new town hall with the winning design.

The Olympic Games

Put the verbs in brackets into the present simple passive, the past simple passive, the present perfect passive or the future passive.

Do you know how often the Olympic Games ▶ *are held* (hold)? They 1_____ (hold) every four years. The first Olympic Games 2_____ (hold) at Olympia, in ancient Greece, nearly 3,000 years ago. The tradition 3_____ (continue) from 776 BC to AD 393. Even wars 4_____ (postpone), so that everyone could travel safely to the Games. The Games 5_____ (ban) in 394.

In 1890 the modern Games 6_____ (found) by a Frenchman called Baron de Coubertin in Athens.

Originally, the Games 7_____ (set up) for amateurs. Amateurs are people who 8_____ (not pay) to play the sport whereas professionals 9_____ (pay). Since 1984 some professional athletes, such as football players, 10_____ (allow) to take part.

Before the Games begin, the Olympic torch 11_____ (light) at Olympus by a mirror reflecting the sun. Then it 12_____ (carry) by runners to the city where the Games 13_____ (hold). Sometimes by the time the last runner enters the stadium, the torch 14_____ (carry) half-way round the world.

Do you know where the next Olympic Games 15_____ (hold)?

22 The plane is being repaired

The passive: continuous and infinitive forms

The Bells have taken Trig to the airport.

JENNY Look, Trig, that plane **is being repaired**.

NICK And that Airbus **is being re-fuelled**.

JENNY And over there passengers **are being taken** to the 747 **by bus**.

TRIG Things are so complicated here. My spaceship was much easier to . . .

NICK . . . crash?

Grammar lesson

The passive: continuous forms

The passive is often used in the present continuous and in the past continuous.

> **am/are/is** + **being** + past participle
>
> **was/were** + **being** + past participle

The present continuous passive shows us that something is taking place now.

> Active Mechanics **are re-fuelling** the plane.
> Passive *The plane **is being re-fuelled**.*

The past continuous passive shows us that something was taking place at a stated or known time in the past.

> Active Mechanics **were re-fuelling** the plane.
> Passive *The plane **was being re-fuelled** when they arrived.*

We can use **by** + person/thing if we wish to say who or what did the action.
> ▶ *They are being taken **by bus**.*

The passive: infinitive form

We form the passive infinitive with **be** + past participle. Verbs such as **can**, **must**, **may**, **might**, **have to**, **should** often come before it.
> ▶ *Planes **have to be serviced** regularly.*

---

1 What is being done?

What is being done at the airport? Complete the sentences by putting the verbs in brackets in the present continuous passive.

▶ Someone's ticket *is being checked* (check).

1 Someone's luggage _____ (weigh).

2 Now labels _____ (stick o

3 Now the cases _____ (pu onto the conveyor belt.

4 A flight _____ (announc over the loudspeaker.

5 Passports _____ (check).

6 Passengers _____ (drive) to the aircraft by bus.

2 I protest!

Mrs Neal is angry. She is complaining to the mayor of Merton.
Put the sentences into the present continuous passive.

▶ You are wasting too much money.
   Too much money is being wasted.
▶ You are not improving education.
   Education is not being improved.

1 You are not helping old people.
2 You are spending money on the wrong things.
3 You are not helping unemployed people.
4 You are doing nothing against crime.
5 You are not cleaning the streets.
6 You are wasting money on dinners and parties.
7 You are building too many offices.
8 You are not improving the health service.
9 You are doing nothing against pollution.
10 You are not lowering taxes.

3 The old house

One day, Jenny noticed that jobs were being done to an old house in Park Street.
Look at the picture and use the past continuous passive of the words from the box to write what was being done.

build	deliver	plant
wash	take away	put up
cut	paint ✓	repair

▶ The door *was being painted.*
1 The grass _____
2 The rubbish _____
3 A garage _____
4 The fence _____
5 The windows _____
6 A nesting box _____
7 Trees _____
8 Furniture _____

4 The environment: what can be done?

What can be done to make the Earth a safer and better place?

We should clean up the air.

ANN

We mustn't put waste into seas and rivers.

TONY

We should protect animals in danger.

BETH

We must change people's attitudes towards the environment.

KATE

We could use more solar energy.

PAUL

Governments ought to make tough laws against litter.

MAX

We shouldn't treat food with chemicals.

MARY

We can save more energy and water.

JOHN

We must find ways of preventing oil spills.

TINA

We should ban cars which use leaded petrol.

JOE

We shouldn't use products which damage the ozone layer.

LIZ

We ought to stop cigarette advertising.

DAVE

a What did they say?
Make the sentences passive.

▶ ANN   *The air should be cleaned up.*

▶ TONY   *Waste mustn't be put into seas and rivers.*

1 BETH   _____

2 KATE   _____

3 PAUL   _____

4 MAX   _____

5 MARY   _____

6 JOHN   _____

7 TINA   _____

8 JOE   _____

9 LIZ   _____

10 DAVE _____

b Think of some more things that **can**/**could**/
must etc. be done to save our planet. Write a
short paragraph in the passive.

---

5 Don't be so impatient!

Nick often has great plans but he doesn't always
have the patience to follow things through.
Use the words from the box to tell Nick what **has
to** be done before he can do these things.

exams/pass	tickets/buy
parents' permission/give	notes/learn ✓
£500/save	special maps/buy
darkroom/build	skis/buy
visa/obtain	

Nick wants to . . .

▶ write music
   The notes have to be learned before you can write music.

1 take skiing lessons
2 go on a school trip
3 go to Nepal
4 go to university
5 go to the rock concert
6 buy a mountain bike
7 trek through the mountains
8 develop photos

23 I want to be a doctor Verbs with **to** + infinitive

JENNY   What do you **want to** be?

JANE   Dad **wants me to** be a dentist but **I want to** be a doctor. I'm **learning to** do first aid. It won't be easy, but I have **decided to** work hard at school. What about you? What **would** you **like to** do?

JENNY   Well, **I like reading**. **I would like to** study languages and literature. **I hope to** go to university. Then **I would like to** work abroad for a while. Uncle Joe has **offered to** help me. He could **help me to** get a job in the States.

JANE   Will your parents **allow you to** leave England?

JENNY   Why not? They **would prefer me to** stay here, but it's up to me. And what about Ben?

JANE   He has **decided to become** Prime Minister . . .

Grammar lesson

Verbs with **to** + infinitive

1   We use **to** + infinitive after these verbs:

afford	learn	plan
agree	manage	promise
decide	offer	want
hope		

▶   *I want to be a doctor.*

2   We can use an object (**you, me, Ben** etc.) + **to** + infinitive after these verbs:

allow	invite	teach
ask	prefer	want
help		

▶   *They would **prefer me to stay** here.*
     *Will they **allow you to leave** England?*

3   After **would like/love/prefer/hate** we use **to** + infinitive.
▶   *I would like to study languages.*

But when there is no **would**, we often use the **ing** form after **like, love, prefer** and **hate**.
▶   *I like studying languages.*

1 What do you want to be?

I want to be a mechanic. I like repairing cars. I would like to have my own garage one day. I don't want to go to university. My uncle has offered to give me a job at his garage.

MAX

MARION

I hope to study biology and chemistry. I love doing experiments. I would like to be a research scientist one day. I hope I manage to get a job at a university.

We can't afford to buy many things at home, so I would like to have a job that pays well – like a pop star. I'm learning to play the guitar – I'm pretty good. I would love to buy a big house for my family.

DAVE

JILL

I don't like being indoors. I would hate to have a job in an office. I would prefer to be a gardener or a game warden. I have decided to leave school next year. I don't want to do any more exams.

a Say the answers to the questions in full sentences.

▶ What does Max want to be?
   He wants to be a mechanic.
▶ What would Dave love to buy?
   He would love to buy a big house for his family.

1 Who wants to be a research scientist?
2 What is Dave learning to play?
3 Who doesn't want to do any more exams?
4 What would Marion like to get?
5 What would Dave like to be?
6 What does Marion hope to study?
7 Who would prefer to have an outdoor job?
8 What has Jill decided to do?
9 What would Max like to have one day?
10 What has Max's uncle offered to do?

b Complete the sentences with the verbs in brackets. Use **to** + infinitive or an **ing** form.

Max has decided ▶ *to become* (become) a mechanic, because he likes ▶ *repairing* (repair) cars.

Max's uncle has offered ¹_____ (give) him a job, but he would like ²_____ (have) his own garage one day.

Marion wants ³_____ (be) a research scientist because she likes ⁴_____ (do) experiments. She would like ⁵_____ (go) to university. She hopes ⁶_____ (study) biology and chemistry.

Jill would love ⁷_____ (have) an outdoor job because she likes ⁸_____ (work) with animals. She doesn't like ⁹_____ (stay) indoors. She has decided ¹⁰_____ (leave) school next year. She would love ¹¹_____ (be) a game warden or a gardener.

Dave is learning ¹²_____ (play) the guitar. He hopes ¹³_____ (become) a pop star, because he likes ¹⁴_____ (write) music. He wants ¹⁵_____ (earn) a lot of money because he would like ¹⁶_____ (buy) a big house for his family.

c What do/don't you like doing?
What would/wouldn't you like to be?
Write a short paragraph.

2 What about you?

Say eight sentences about yourself using the **to** +
infinitive form. Use words from the lists or use
your own ideas.

▶ *I have decided to do all the housework.*

have offered	buy a motor bike/car/boat
can (not) afford	do all the housework
have decided (not)	stay out late
hope	become a film star/rock star/international model
have promised (not)	spend lots of money on clothes/shoes
have (not) agreed	read every play by Shakespeare
would (not) like	do nothing all day
(don't) want	live in the mountains
can (not) manage	study physics at university
	write a book about centipedes
	become an opera singer
	learn every word in the English language
	play professional basketball

3 Conflicts

What do they want to do?
What do other people want them to do?
Write the answers.

▶ JENNY   I'm going to the cinema on
Saturday.

JANE   Why don't you go to the bowling
alley with me instead?

*Jenny wants to go to the cinema, but
Jane wants her to go to the bowling alley.*

1   TOM   I'm going to the music shop.

NICK   Why don't you go to the fun-fair
with me instead?

_____

2   JANE   I'm staying at home tonight.

AMANDA   That's boring. Go to the basketball
game with me.

_____

3   BEN   I want to go to the air show on
Sunday.

TOM   Can't you go with me on Saturday?

_____

4   JENNY   I'm going to watch television now.

AMANDA   Let's go to the snack bar instead.

_____

5   BEN   I'm going to give my old computer
games to my cousins.

AMANDA   Oh? Can't you give them to me?

_____

6   MIKE   I'm going to visit my friends in
London tomorrow.

SUE   Can't you visit them next week
instead?

_____

7   JANE   I'm going to the swimming pool.

BEN   But you said you would help me
with my chemistry.

_____

4 I'd like them to . . .

What would you like other people to do?
Say two things that you would like each of these
people to do:

your friend
your parents (father/mother)
your brother/sister

▶ *I would like my friend to go to town with me on Saturday.*
▶ *I would like my mother to stop complaining about my clothes.*

---

5 Mystery message

Nick has found this strange message in his pocket.
Can you work out what it says? Write it in the
space below.

Clue: cross out these letters

b1 ✓   i1   a3   c1   k4   b4   d3   k2   d1   m1
i3   h3   j4   c2   e4   m2   h2   l2   i4   a4

	a	b	c	d	e	f	g	h	i	j	k	l	m
1	I	X	W	O	W	A	N	T	O	Y	O	U	R
2	T	O	O	M	E	E	T	O	M	E	N	K	O
3	T	I	N	O	T	H	E	M	O	P	A	R	K
4	T	H	A	T	O	T	E	N	N	I	S	.	

Message: *I*

24 If you hadn't …   Conditional sentences type 3; **may**, **might** for possibility

JENNY   Nick, catch the ball! Oh no, look what you've done. You've broken the lamp.

NICK   If you **hadn't** thrown the ball so high, I **wouldn't have knocked** it off the table. It wasn't really my fault.

JENNY   Well, whose fault was it? If you **had looked**, you **would have seen** it .

NICK   It's too late now. We **may** be able to stick it together. Then Mum **might not** notice.

JENNY   It's too risky. She **might** want to use it. Why don't we just tell her what happened?

NICK   And get my pocket money stopped again? Not likely! Where's the glue?

Grammar lesson

Conditional sentences type 3

We use **if** + past perfect + **would have** + past participle for unreal situations in the past.

if clause	*Main clause*
past perfect	**would have** + past participle

We imagine a condition or situation in the past which was impossible or didn't happen.
- ▶ *If you* **had looked**, *. . .* (but you didn't look)

When the **if** clause comes first, we usually use a comma (,) after it. We can also put the main clause first.
- ▶ *I* **wouldn't have knocked** *it off the table if you* **hadn't thrown** *the ball so high.*

may, **might** for possibility

We use **may** or **might** + infinitive without **to** to talk about something that is possible now or in the future. Both mean 'perhaps'.
- ▶ *We* **may be able to** *stick it.*
  (= Perhaps we can stick it.)
  She **might not** *notice.*
  (= Perhaps she will not notice.)

1 Will you lend me your bike?

Complete the sentences with the words in brackets in the past perfect or with **would have** + past participle.

BEN   Will you lend me your bike? I have to get to basketball training in five minutes.

NICK   The last time I lent it to you, you got a flat tyre and didn't repair it.

BEN   Well, I ▶ *wouldn't have got* (not get) a flat tyre if you ▶ *had put* (put) enough air in it.

NICK   That's not true. You rode straight over some broken glass.

BEN   Well, I [1]_____ (not ride) over the glass if someone [2]_____ (left) it all over the road. Besides, I [3]_____ (go) round the glass, if a car [4]_____ (not come) from the other direction.

NICK   Well, you could have stopped.

BEN   I [5]_____ (stop) if the brakes [6]_____ (not fail).

NICK   Well, you should have checked the brakes before you started. I [7]_____ (not lend) you my bike if I [8]_____ (know) that the brakes weren't working.

2 Heroes

Look at these newspaper headlines about people who have done heroic acts.
Write sentences about them with the words provided and **if**.

▶ **Joe Smith saved family from fire**

    not hear their cries   not find them

If he hadn't heard their cries, he wouldn't have found them.

1 **Constable Pierce pulled woman from exploding car**

    arrive one minute later   be too late

_____

_____

2 **Christie Combe saved cat from tree**

    not find a ladder   not be able to save it

_____

_____

3 **Ken Spudgen warned police of hold-up**

    Walkman not stop working   not hear the thieves' plan

_____

_____

4 **Susan Adams found lost child**

    not go jogging   not find the child

_____

_____

5 **Jimmy Bond warned motorists of collapsed bridge**

    not walk along river   not see the bridge

_____

_____

6 **Karen Wright saved man from drowning**

    not taken a first aid course   not know what to do

_____

_____

3 Accidents

The people in the doctor's waiting room have all had accidents. Read what happened. Then make sentences with **if**, like this:

▶ Mr Jones fell off his bicycle.
He broke his arm.
If he hadn't fallen off his bicycle, he wouldn't have broken his arm.

1 Mrs King fell off a ladder.
She broke her arm.

2 Mrs Fox dropped the iron.
She burned her hand.

3 Mr Brown slipped on a banana skin.
He twisted his ankle.

4 Mr Bell walked into a lamp post.
He bumped his head.

5 Mrs Green fell down the stairs.
She hurt her knee.

6 Miss Page didn't fasten her seat belt.
She broke her nose.

7 Mr Grey didn't pay attention.
He shut the door on his finger.

8 Jimmy tried to do a trick.
He got his head stuck in a chair.

4   Are you influenced by advertising?

Jenny has asked people if they are influenced by advertising. Here are some of the answers.

No, I don't think so. I bought this watch last week. I had seen a commercial for it on TV, but it's a good, reliable watch. I would have bought it even if I hadn't seen the commercial.

BILL

Yes, I'm sure that I am. Yesterday I bought these trainers. If I hadn't read about them, I would have chosen a cheaper pair. I wouldn't have paid so much money if the ad hadn't influenced me.

ROB

I think everybody is influenced by advertising. Last week I bought a new shampoo. If I hadn't seen a magazine ad for the product, I wouldn't have tried it.

PAT

No. I buy whatever is the cheapest. But it's not always a good idea. Last week I bought a cheap red jumper and the colour came out. If I had bought a better jumper, it would have kept its colour.

ANN

a   What did they say? Read the sentences and say if they are true or false. Correct the false statements.

▶ Bill wouldn't have bought the watch if he hadn't seen a commercial on TV.
False. He would have bought the watch anyway.

1   Rob would have bought a cheaper pair of trainers if he hadn't read an ad for the expensive pair.
2   Pat would have tried the new shampoo, even if she hadn't read about it.
3   Ann's jumper would have lost its colour, even if she had paid more.
4   Rob would have bought the expensive trainers anyway.
5   Bill would have bought the watch even if he hadn't seen the commercial.
6   Rob would have paid more money if he hadn't seen the ad.

b   Think of the commercials you have seen and the things you have bought recently. Think of something you bought because you had seen a commercial on TV or an advertisement in a magazine.
If you hadn't seen the products advertised, would you have bought them anyway?
Write a short paragraph.

Situations

Say what you would have done if these things had happened to you.

▶ Claire saw a man steal something in a shop. She told a shop assistant what she had seen.
If I had seen someone steal something, I would have done the same thing. OR
If I had seen someone steal something, I would not have said anything.

1 Jim saw a car accident. He didn't help immediately, but he ran into a shop to telephone an ambulance.

2 Mike heard a friend tell a lie. He didn't say anything. Later he asked the friend why he had lied.

3 Susan found a purse in the street. There was only a little money in it and no important papers or cards. There was no one in the street. She kept the money.

4 A stranger asked Pat for some money in the street. The stranger said he had to go somewhere urgently by taxi and had forgotten his wallet. Pat gave him the money and her telephone number.

5 A TV reporter was asking passers-by their opinion about TV programmes. David wanted to be on television, so he combed his hair and went up to the reporter.

6 Fears

Give reasons why some people don't like the following things. What do they think **might** happen? Say your answers.

▶ Some people don't like flying.
They think the plane might crash.

1 Some people don't like going in lifts.
2 Some people don't like driving in cities.
3 Some people don't like dogs.
4 Some people don't like being in the dark.
5 Some people don't like heights.
6 Some people don't like snakes.

7 About you

Say five things that you **may/might** (**not**) do when you leave school.

Use these ideas or think of your own:

go to university
go abroad
get a job in England for a year
get married
go to Hollywood
join the army
become a professional football player

▶ *I may go to university.*
I might not stay in this country.
I may get a job abroad . . .

25 Play it more slowly Comparison of adverbs; **wish** + past perfect

Mike and his band are practising a new song. Nick is listening.

MIKE   Stop! It's all wrong. It should be played **more slowly**.

RON   Well, I think we should play it **faster**. And what's going on, Pete? You're playing **worse** than yesterday.

PETE   Look who's talking. You're not doing any **better** yourself.

MIKE   Relax. We'll just have to work **harder** at it. Sorry, Nick. I **wish** you **had heard** us last night. We were pretty good. In fact, we played **the best** ever.

NICK   You sounded fine to me. But wasn't it a bit loud?

RON   We play **more quietly** when the neighbour starts banging on the wall.

Grammar lesson

Comparison of adverbs

Adverbs of manner describe how we do things (**carefully**, **badly**, **slowly**, **well** etc.).

We use **more** and **the most** to compare adverbs ending with **-ly**.

quick	**more** quickly	**most** quickly
slowly	**more** slowly	**most** slowly

▶ *We play **more quietly** when the neighbour starts banging on the wall.*

We compare irregular adverbs in the same way as adjectives with **-er/-est**.

fast	fast**er**	fast**est**
hard	hard**er**	hard**est**
early	earl**ier**	earl**iest**

▶ *We'll have to work **harder** at it.*

Here are some more irregular adverbs:

well	**better**	**best**
badly	**worse**	**worst**
much	**more**	**most**
little	**less**	**least**

▶ *You're not doing any **better** yourself.*
*We played **the best** we've ever played.*

We use **than** to make comparisons in the same way as with adjectives.
▶ *We're playing **worse than** yesterday.*

wish + past perfect

We use **wish** + past perfect to talk about something in the past that we regret. We cannot change what happened or didn't happen.
▶ *I **wish** you **had heard** us last night.* (but you didn't hear us last night)

1 Do it well

Complete the table with adverbs in the correct form.

adverb	comparative	superlative
slowly	▶ *more slowly*	most slowly
fast	▶ *faster*	1
well	2	best
easily	3	4
quietly	5	6
7	worse	8
much	9	10
11	more carefully	12
little	13	14
thoroughly	15	16
17	earlier	18
19	20	hardest

Which ones could you do the easiest – I mean most easily?

---

2 Faster than ever before

Complete the advertisements by putting an adverb from the box in the comparative form. Sometimes more than one answer is possible.

well	gently
fast	thoroughly ✓
quickly	soundly
easily ✓	

▶ The new **Magic Brush** will clean your teeth _more thoroughly_ than ever before!

▶ **Spotless** makes your spots disappear _more easily_ !

1 **SOFTWOOL** washes your pullovers _____ than any other washing powder.

2 **Dew soap** will cleanse your face _____ than ever before.

3 **Deepsleep** will help you to sleep _____ than you thought possible.

4 **BREATHEASY** will make colds disappear _____ than any other medicine.

5 With **Kilos-off** you will lose weight _____ than you dared to imagine.

6 With the new **Pop up** camera your photos will turn out _____ than ever before!

3 Resolutions

a At the beginning of a new year Ben always makes resolutions to do things better.
Complete his resolutions for this year with adverbs from the box in comparative form. Sometimes more than one answer is possible.

early	quietly
neatly	regularly
little ✓	much
hard	good
seriously	

▶ I will sleep —————————— in class.

1 I will take school ——————————.

2 I will go to bed ——————————.

3 I will write ——————————.

4 I will do my homework ——————————.

5 I will behave —————————— at school.

6 I will train —————————— for the school football team.

7 I will play my radio ——————————.

8 I will work —————————— for exams.

b Write three resolutions. What will you do better next year? Use the comparative form of the adverbs in (**a**) or others.

▶ ——————————————————————

————————————————————————

————————————————————————

————————————————————————

I will work less. I will eat more quickly.

4 I wish . . .

What do they wish they had or hadn't done? Say sentences with **wish** + past perfect.

▶ Ben spent all his money on a camera.
He wishes he hadn't spent all his money on a camera.

1 Jenny bought a skirt that she didn't really like.
2 Jane sold her Walkman.
3 Tom lost his bicycle lock.
4 Nick didn't enter the graffiti competition.
5 Amanda didn't buy the leather belt that she liked.
6 Mike moved the furniture around in his room.
7 Jenny missed two episodes of her favourite soap opera.
8 Ben didn't go to Max's party.

5 What do you wish you had done?

Think of what you did or didn't do last week. Are there things you wish you had done or hadn't done?
Say three things.

▶ *I wish I had gone to town last Saturday.*
▶ *I wish I hadn't torn my best shirt.*

6 It's too late . . .

Read the sentences and write what they wish they had
or had not done.

▶ I didn't ask what her name was.

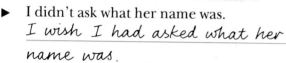
I wish I had asked what her name was.

1   I didn't ask her where she lived.

2   I told her that she had a funny voice.

3   I didn't tell her that I usually come here on Saturdays.

4   I left early.

5   I wasn't nice to him.

6   I pretended not to be interested.

7   I told him I was here with someone else.

8   I didn't tell him my name.

26 Do you want to go . . . ? Verbs with **to** + infinitive or **ing** form

JENNY   Hi. How are you?

AMANDA   Bored. What are we going to do today?

JENNY   Well, do you **want to play** tennis?

AMANDA   My racket's broken and I can't **afford to buy** another one.

JENNY   Do you **feel like swimming**?

AMANDA   I **can't stand swimming**. You get all wet.

JENNY   Jane **has invited us to go** riding with her.

AMANDA   I don't know **how to ride**. Tom **offered to teach** me once but the horse kicked me as soon as I went near. **I refused to carry on**.

JENNY   Nick **wanted us to go** to the zoo with him . . .

AMANDA   I'm **against keeping** animals in zoos. I **stopped visiting** zoos two years ago.

JENNY   I don't know **what to suggest**. You don't **want to do** anything.

AMANDA   Exactly! That's why I'm so bored.

Grammar lesson

Verbs with **to** + infinitive

- We use **to** + infinitive after **afford, agree, decide, hope, manage, offer, promise, refuse, seem, want** etc.
  - ▶ *I can't **afford to buy** another one.*

- We use a **to** + infinitive after the question words **when, what, where, how** etc. (but not after **why**).
  - ▶ *I don't know **what to do**.*

- We use **to** + infinitive after some verbs + objects (**me, Tom**). For example, **advise, ask, expect, help, invite, order, persuade, tell, want** etc.
  - ▶ *Nick **wanted us to go** to the zoo with him.*

Verbs with **ing** form

- We always use the **ing** form of a verb which follows **avoid, dislike, enjoy, feel like, finish, can't help, don't mind, risk, can't stand, suggest** etc.
  - ▶ *Do you **feel like swimming**? I **can't stand swimming**.*

- We always use the **ing** form of a verb which follows a preposition.
  - ▶ *I'm **against keeping** animals in zoos. She is **for stopping** pollution.*

to + infinitive or **ing** form?

After some verbs we can use **to** + infinitive or an **ing** form without an important change in meaning. These verbs are **begin, continue, hate, like, love, start** and a few others.
- ▶ *I hate swimming.   I hate to swim.*

After **stop** and **remember** we can use a **to** + infinitive or an **ing** form, but there is a change in meaning.
- ▶ *I stopped visiting zoos. (= I don't visit zoos now.)*
  I stopped to visit a zoo. (= purpose, in order to visit a zoo)
- ▶ *I remember buying the tickets. (= I remember that I bought . . .)*
  I remembered to buy the tickets. (= I didn't forget to buy . . .)

1 I want to work

a Put the verbs into the correct lists.

enjoy ✓	risk	dislike
want ✓	don't mind	refuse
promise	can't stand	offer
can't help	hope	seem
decide		

▶ *want*
_____
_____
_____
_____
_____   } **+ to work**

▶ *enjoy*
_____
_____
_____
_____
_____   } **+ working**

b Work with a partner.
Your partner says a verb from (**a**) above.
You must say a correct sentence with the verb
before your partner has counted to ten.

▶ PARTNER *'Promise'. One, two, three,*
                    four . . .
   YOU   *I promise to help you with your*
                    homework.

Now you choose a verb for your partner and
start counting to ten.

2 Thomas Edison

Complete the story about the inventor Thomas
Edison with **to** + infinitive or an **ing** form.

Thomas Edison was one of the greatest inventors
of all time. But as a child, he didn't enjoy
▶ *going*_____ (go) to school.

When Edison was only seven, the headmaster
decided ¹_____ (expel) him because he
refused ²_____ (do) his school work. He
only went to school for three months,
but he never stopped ³_____ (learn).

His mother managed ⁴_____ (teach)
him the most important things, and she
persuaded him ⁵_____ (read) about
science. He didn't mind ⁶_____ (stay)
at home and he enjoyed ⁷_____ (read).
He couldn't afford ⁸_____ (buy)
the books he needed, so at twelve he began
⁹_____ (sell) newspapers and sweets in
trains.

He loved ¹⁰_____ (do) experiments,
and he set up a laboratory in the luggage van of
a train. When he was older, he invented the
phonograph and the light bulb.

Do you know the story of Edison and the egg?
He wanted ¹¹_____ (boil) his egg
himself, so he asked his housekeeper
¹²_____ (bring) an egg and a pan of
hot water to his laboratory. She told him
¹³_____ (not forget) about the egg.
He seemed ¹⁴_____ (listen) to her.
But when she returned half an hour later he
was boiling his watch and timing it with the egg.

3 First aid

What do you know about first aid?
Use words from each list to make eight sentences.

▶ *I know what to do if someone faints.*
▶ *I don't know how to help someone who has swallowed poison.*

I know	how	to do if someone faints
I don't know	where	to help someone who has swallowed poison
I'm not sure	what	to bandage a cut
I'd have to find out	when	to do with a broken arm
		to feel someone's pulse
		to stop bleeding
		to do with a burn
		to treat a person in shock
		to move an unconscious person
		to do if someone is choking

But I've only got a sore finger . . .

---

4 A questionnaire about smoking

a Use the verbs in brackets with **to** + infinitive
or an **ing** form to complete the questions.
Then put a √ in one of the boxes.

		yes	no	not sure
▶ Are you for _smoking_ (smoke) in public places?		☐	☐	☑
1 Would you advise people _____ (stop)?		☐	☐	☐
2 Are you against _____ (advertise) cigarettes?		☐	☐	☐
3 Do you dislike _____ (breathe) other people's smoke?		☐	☐	☐
4 Would you refuse _____ (let) people smoke in a car?		☐	☐	☐
5 Do you mind people _____ (smoke) around you?		☐	☐	☐
6 Do most people start _____ (smoke) too young?		☐	☐	☐
7 Should shopkeepers refuse _____ (sell) cigarettes to children?		☐	☐	☐
8 Can most smokers manage _____ (stop) smoking?		☐	☐	☐
9 Do smokers risk _____ (damage) their health?		☐	☐	☐
10 Are most teenagers persuaded _____ (smoke) by their friends?		☐	☐	☐

b Write your opinion about smoking in a short paragraph.

5 Remember to do it

a Ring the correct answer, then write it in.

▶ Mr Bell used to smoke, but he stopped
smoking ten years ago.

  a smoke
  b to smoke
  ⓒ smoking

1 Mrs Bell must remember _____ the
butcher to order the meat for the weekend.

  a to phone
  b phoning
  c phone

2 On her way home from school, Jenny
stopped _____ to some friends.

  a talking
  b to talk
  c talk

3 The milkman thinks that Mrs Bell forgot to
pay him, but she can remember
_____ the bill.

  a to pay
  b paying
  c pay

4 Mr Blake asked the class to stop
_____.

  a to talk
  b talk
  c talking

5 Nick can remember _____ to school
for the first time.

  a to go
  b go
  c going

6 Ben didn't remember _____ his
bicycle. The brakes still squeak.

  a oiling
  b to oil
  c oil

7 On his way to the station, Mr Bell stopped
_____ a letter.

  a to post
  b post
  c posting

8 Jenny, stop _____ your nails! Don't
be so nervous!

  a biting
  b to bite
  c bite

9 I didn't remember _____ to the
bank. Now I have no money.

  a going
  b go
  c to go

10 Jenny can remember _____ off her
bicycle and _____ her leg when she
was six.

  a to fall, breaking
  b falling, to break
  c falling, breaking

b Write three things that you must remember to
do before next weekend.

▶ _I must remember to buy a stamp._

_____

_____

c Write three things that you can remember doing
when you were a small child.

▶ _I remember falling down the stairs._

_____

_____

_____

Future perfect simple and continuou
Present simple for future time

Jenny and Jane have come to watch the Merton Marathon.

JANE   What time is it?

JENNY   It's nine o'clock.

JANE   By ten thirty the runners **will have finished**.

JENNY   No. They **won't have finished** by then. The women **will not** even **have started** by then.

JANE   What time **do** they **start**?

JENNY   The men's race **starts** at nine thirty and the women's race **starts** at eleven thirty.

JANE   By the time they arrive, we **will have been waiting** for hours.

JENNY   Yes, and they **will have been running** for hours.

Grammar lesson

Future perfect simple

We form the future perfect simple with **will have** + past participle.

▶ *By ten thirty, they **will have** finished.*

We use the future perfect simple to talk about actions that will be completed at a particular time in the future.

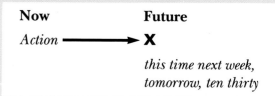

Now	**Future**
Action ⟶	**X**
	this time next week, tomorrow, ten thirty

The future perfect is often used with **by** (= up to) + point of time (**by then, by next week, by the year 2000** etc.).

▶ *They **won't have finished** by then.*

Future perfect continuous

We form the future perfect continuous with **will have been** + **ing** form.

▶ *We **will have been waiting** for hours.*

We use the future perfect continuous for actions that start in the future and continue to happen up to a particular time in the future. It is often used with **for** + length of time (**for hours** etc.).

Present simple for future time

We use the present simple with a future meaning to talk about fixed or arranged times, for example, timetables and official programmes.

▶ *The men's race **starts** at nine thirty.*

1 Find the answers

Find the future perfect simple and the future perfect continuous forms in the list below. Write the letter in brackets in the right box to find the answers to the questions below.

	Future perfect simple	Future perfect cont.
he will have left (E) ▶	E	
he will have been reading (F) ▶		F
it will be raining (P)		
she won't have been waiting (I)		
they will have finished (D)		
will it have landed? (I)		
she will be invited (Z)		
will he have been working? (F)		
it will have been raining (T)		
will we have arrived? (N)		
he will be reading (A)		
I won't have been watching (Y)		
he won't have started (B)		
they will have written (U)		
we will have been learning (T)		
I will have gone (R)		
he won't be asked (S)		
you will have done (G)		
will they have been skiing? (W)		
she will have been talking (O)		
we will have left (H)		

Future perfect simple:
What is the capital of Scotland?

_ _ _ _ _ _ _ _ _

Future perfect continuous:
How many states are there in the USA?

_ _ _ _ _ - _ _ _

2 Pocket money

Do you save some of your pocket money, or do you spend it all? This is how much Jenny and Nick and their friends save or spend in a week:

	saves	spends
Jenny	£2	£2
Nick	50p	£3.50
Tom	£1	£4
Amanda	£2.50	£1.50
Jane	£1.50	£2.50
Ben	nothing	£3.50

Imagine that today is the first day of February. Answer the questions in full sentences.

▶ How much will Jenny have saved by the end of February?
By the end of February Jenny will have saved £8.

▶ How much will Nick have spent by the middle of March?
By the middle of March Nick will have spent £21.

1 How much will Ben have saved by the end of February?

2 How much pocket money will Jane have received by the end of February?

3 How much will Amanda have saved by the middle of March?

4 How much will Jane have spent by the middle of March?

5 How much pocket money will Nick have received by the middle of March?

6 How much will Nick have saved by the middle of March?

7 How much will Tom have saved by the end of March?

8 How much will Jenny have spent by the end of March?

9 How much pocket money will Tom have received by the end of March?

10 How much will Ben have spent by the end of March?

11 Who will have saved the most by the end of March?

12 Who will have spent the most by the end of March?

3 What will they have done?

Write **a**, **b** or **c** in the gap and read the completed sentences.

▶ By the weekend they _C_ the next issue of their newspaper.

   a will have been completing
   b have completed
   ⓒ will have completed

1 By Wednesday afternoon, Tom _____ four people.

   a will have interviewed
   b will interview
   c will be interviewed

2 By tomorrow night Jenny _____ four articles.

   a will be written
   b will have written
   c won't have been writing

3 When the newspaper comes out, they _____ on it for six weeks.

   a will work
   b will have been working
   c won't have been working

4 They hope that by the end of next week they _____ 2,000 copies.

   a will be sold
   b will have sold
   c won't have sold

5 Nick hopes that by the end of the year they _____ rich and famous.

   a won't become
   b became
   c will have become

6 By next month, Amanda _____ seven articles.

   a will have written
   b will have been writing
   c will write

4 About you

Write the answers in full sentences.
Use **for** + length of time.

▶ How long will you have been learning English by the end of this school year?
By the end of this school year, I will ha
been learning English for three years.

1 How long will you have been living in your town by next summer?

_____

_____

2 How long will you have been living in your house or flat by next year?

_____

_____

3 How long will you have known your English teacher by the end of this school year?

_____

_____

4 How long will you have known your best frie by next summer?

_____

_____

5 How long will you have been watching your favourite TV programme by the end of this year?

_____

_____

6 How long will you have been attending your present school by the end of the school year?

_____

_____

5   A trip to Cornwall

Mr Blake is taking his class to Cornwall. Look at his itinerary and complete the questions or answers in the present simple.

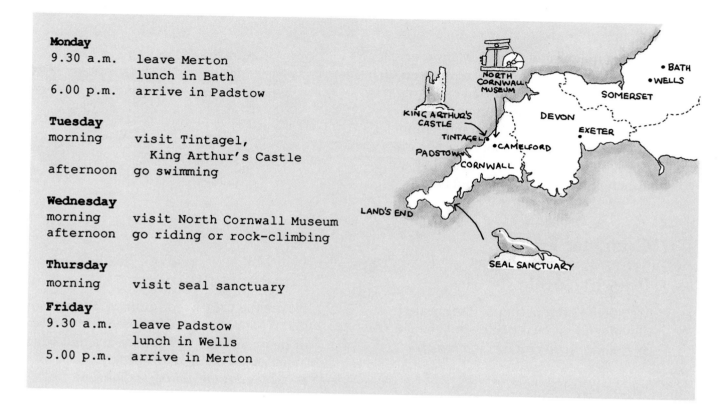

Monday
9.30 a.m.   leave Merton
               lunch in Bath
6.00 p.m.   arrive in Padstow

Tuesday
morning   visit Tintagel,
                  King Arthur's Castle
afternoon   go swimming

Wednesday
morning   visit North Cornwall Museum
afternoon   go riding or rock-climbing

Thursday
morning   visit seal sanctuary

Friday
9.30 a.m.   leave Padstow
               lunch in Wells
5.00 p.m.   arrive in Merton

Questions	Answers
▶ When do we leave Merton?	We leave Merton on Monday at 9.30.
▶ *Where do we have lunch?*	In Bath.
1 _____	We arrive at about 6 in the evening.
2 When do we visit the seal sanctuary?	_____
3 _____	On Wednesday morning.
4 When do we go rock-climbing?	_____
5 _____	On Tuesday afternoon.
6 When do we go to Tintagel?	_____
7 When do we go riding?	_____
8 _____	On Friday morning at 9.30.
9 _____	In Wells.
10 When do we arrive home?	_____

Amanda, Nick and Jane **have gone** to Cornwall on a school trip. So far, they **have been having** a great time. There **has** only **been** one small problem.

Yesterday, they **visited** a castle. Many tourists **visit** it every year. Amanda **had never seen** such an old castle before. She **started** exploring it by herself. Then it **happened**. Amanda **was looking** for secret passages in a small room when the wind **blew** the door shut. She **was** trapped. She **had been shouting** for half an hour before Nick and Jane **found** her.

Today they **are visiting** the North Cornwall Museum. They **are taking** a guided tour. Amanda **is staying** close to the rest of the class.

Grammar lesson

Present simple

We use the present simple for repeated actions and for facts that do not change.
▶ *Many tourists **visit** the castle every year.*

Past simple

We use the past simple for an action which started and finished in the past, often with an expression of past time (**last year, in 1969** etc.).
▶ *Yesterday they **visited** a castle.*

Present perfect simple

We use the present perfect simple for a completed action at an unknown or unstated time (without a time reference).
▶ *They **have gone** to Cornwall. (We don't know when – and it isn't important.)*

Past perfect simple

We use the past perfect simple for a completed action in the past which started and finished before another action in the past.
▶ *Amanda **had** never **seen** such an old castle before. She **started** exploring it.*

Present continuous

We use the present continuous for an action that is happening at the moment of speaking or for an action that happens at a time which includes the moment of speaking.
▶ *Today they **are visiting** the museum.*

Past continuous

We use the past continuous for an action which was happening when another action started.
▶ *Amanda **was looking** for secret passages when the wind **blew** the door shut.*

Present perfect continuous

We use the present perfect continuous for an action which began in the past and continues up to the present. The action may be completed or not completed.
▶ *So far, they **have been having** a great time.*

Past perfect continuous

We use the past perfect continuous for a past action which continued until another past action happened.
▶ *She **had been shouting** for half an hour before Nick and Jane **found** her.*

1 The first man in space

Cross out the wrong verb forms and read about the first man in space.

It all | ▶ began/~~has begun~~ | on April the 12th, 1961. The Russian astronaut, Yuri Gagarin, | 1 has been woken up/was woken up | by his doctor. After he | 2 was eating/had eaten | a breakfast of meat paste, marmalade and coffee, his doctor | 3 gave/has given | him a medical examination.

At 7 o'clock Gagarin | 4 walked/walks | up the platform of Vostok 1. He | 5 waved/was waving | goodbye to all those who | 6 had come/were coming | to see him. Then Gagarin | 7 disappeared/was disappearing | into the spaceship. Finally, at 7.58, he | 8 has announced/announced | that he was ready for take-off.

Gagarin's flight | 9 was lasting/lasted | only 108 minutes. During the flight he had the feeling that he | 10 hung/was hanging | in the air. His atlas, pencil and notebook | 11 floated/have floated | around him in the cabin. Vostock | 12 started/has started | its return flight at 8.25, after it | 13 had orbited/was orbiting | the earth once.

Back on Earth, a farm woman and her granddaughter, who | 14 had seen/were seeing | the spaceship as it | 15 landed/lands |, were the first people to greet the astronaut. Gagarin | 16 had travelled/was travelling | less than one hour in space, but he | 17 went/has gone | where no man | 18 had gone/was going | before.

2 Famous names in space

Put the verbs in the present simple, present perfect simple or past simple to make correct sentences.

Most people ▶ _have seen_ (see) several rocket launches on television. There ▶ _is_ (be) nothing very unusual about space travel today. Space flights 1_____ (belong) to our modern world, but thirty years ago sending a satellite into space 2_____ (be) very exciting.

3_____ (you hear) of Laika, the unlucky dog which the Russians 4_____ (launch) into space in 1957? She 5_____ (be) the first living creature in space. Unfortunately, she never 6_____ (return). However, a few years later, in 1966, the Russian dogs Weterok and Ugoljok 7_____ (orbit) the Earth 330 times and finally 8_____ (return) safely.

9_____ (you hear) of Valentina Tereshkova? She 10_____ (circle) the Earth 48 times in 1963 – she was the first woman in space.

But there is one name that everybody 11_____ (know) – Neil Armstrong, the first man on the Moon. On the 20th of July 1969, Neil Armstrong and Buzz Aldrin 12_____ (land) on the Moon and the whole world 13_____ (watch) them on television. The astronauts 14_____ (be) 385,000 kilometres from home.

So far, astronauts 15_____ (land) on the Moon only. But will Mars be next?

3 The surprise party

Last week Jenny and Jane organized a big surprise party for Tom's birthday. This is what happened but the events are in the wrong order. Complete the sentences by writing the words in brackets in the past simple or the past continuous. Then write a number in the box to show what order the sentences should be in.

[2] Jenny ▶ _phoned_ (phone) all Tom's friends while he ▶ _was playing_ (play) tennis with Nick.

[ ] When Tom 1_____ (not look) Jenny 2_____ (take) his address book out of his pocket.

[ ] On Saturday morning, Jenny and Jane 3_____ (buy) the food for the party when Tom 4_____ (see) them at the supermarket. But he 5_____ (not guess) what they 6_____ (do).

[ ] Tom 7_____ (cycle) in the park with Nick when all the guests 8_____ (arrive) for the party.

[ ] While Tom 9_____ (walk) up the stairs all his friends suddenly 10_____ (shout), 'Surprise!'

[ ] When Tom 11_____ (arrive) in front of the house with Nick, all his friends 12_____ (hide).

[ ] When Jane 13_____ (return) the address book to Tom's pocket, he 14_____ (plan) an article with Jenny.

4 Test your tenses

How well do you know your tenses? Ring **a**, **b** or **c** and write in the correct answer.

▶ She _hasn't been_ _____ well lately. She looks very pale.

   a wasn't
   b isn't being
  (**c**) hasn't been

1 Amanda _____ many old castles yet.

   a hasn't visited
   b is visiting
   c was visiting

2 Before she had the accident, she _____ a nice time in Cornwall.

   a has had
   b is having
   c had been having

3 In general, Trig _____ hard work and early mornings.

   a doesn't like
   b wasn't liking
   c hadn't been liking

4 I'm sorry, but Nick _____ out for the day.

   a has gone
   b goes
   c was going

5 _____ to the football game tomorrow?

   a Did you come
   b Do you come
   c Are you coming

6 Who was he? She was sure that she _____ him before.

   a has seen
   b had seen
   c is seeing

7 When Nick came in, they _____ about the party.

   a were talking
   b are talking
   c talk

8 Jenny usually _____ her work on time. What's happened?

   a finished
   b finishes
   c has finished

9 I can't hear a thing! Everyone _____ at the same time.

   a talks
   b has been talking
   c is talking

10 Mike _____ his car when it started to rain.

   a was washing
   b washes
   c is washing

11 Nick _____ for the football match all week.

   a has been training
   b is training
   c trains

12 Trig is speaking Triglonian. I _____ him.

   a don't understand
   b wasn't understanding
   c had been understanding

Oxford University Press
Walton Street, Oxford OX2 6DP

Oxford New York
Athens Auckland Bangkok Bombay
Calcutta Cape Town Dar es Salaam Delhi
Florence Hong Kong Istanbul Karachi
Kuala Lumpur Madras Madrid Melbourne
Mexico City Nairobi Paris Singapore
Taipei Tokyo Toronto

and associated companies in
Berlin Ibadan

OXFORD and OXFORD ENGLISH
are trade marks of Oxford University Press.

ISBN 0 19 431363 8
ISBN 0 19 431356 5 (Greek edition)

© Oxford University Press 1993

First published 1993
Sixth impression 1995

Illustrated by Heather Clarke
Typeset in Baskerville by Pentacor PLC

Printed in Hong Kong